THE **BRAND** NEW LEADER

Recognizing the Impact of your Leadership Brand

Dr. Melva B. Robertson

Foreword by Wesley J. Hall, ICD.D

Voted One of Canada's Most Powerful Business People

Publishing, Booking, and Purchasing Information:

The Write Media Group, LLC

www.thewritemediagrp.com

www.melvarobertson.com

Email: administrator@thewritemediagrp.com

Book Editor: Kay M. Bower, DSL, PMP

Koinonia Coaching & Consulting

Foreword: Wesley J. Hall, ICD.D

Executive Chairman & Founder

KSS Group of Companies

ISBN 978-0-578-80406-4

DEDICATION

I dedicate this project to my village—my tribe of parents, grandparents, godparents, aunts, uncles, cousins, friends, colleagues, and other support systems. All of whom, throughout my life, have and continue to pour into me, inspire me, support me, and provide the foundational and consistent example of leadership that has pushed me to pursue my purpose. To you all, who are too numerous to name, I am eternally grateful for your sacrifice, love, and influence.

To my husband, Dereko, and my daughter Aria Jayde, thank you for your love, support, motivation, and patience as I completed this endeavor. Thank you for your encouragement during difficult times and for the laughter that I needed in the midst of the intense moments of this journey. You both sacrificed so much to stand by me, and I am eternally grateful and love you endlessly. Dereko, I am so proud of you, continue to lead and follow your calling! Aria, your spirit inspires me daily. Thank you for teaching me how to love life truly and how to enjoy every moment of it. I pray that we, your parents, can be the positive example for you that so many have been for us. You are destined for greatness and leadership; pursue it boldly!

To my mother, Dr. Florence Bell: You were my first teacher of love, leadership, grace, courage, and perseverance.

Your example has always been the single, best lesson that I could ever learn. More significant than degrees or textbooks, I have learned how to appreciate and embrace both the joys and vicissitudes of life because of you. Thank you for instilling in me an avidity for knowledge, compassion for others, and the true meaning of servant leadership. I love you!

Hilda Walker, you are my earth angel. Saying "I love you" and "thank you" does not convey what I feel from the depths of my heart for you. Ricky and Benita Reed, you are always there. You are great cheerleaders, and I love and appreciate you both. Olivia Dixson, you are beautiful and amazing. I cannot wait to see all that you will become. Let nothing stop you from what God has called you to be! Brandon and Jordan, my brothers: I hope to be an example, a shoulder, listening ear, and voice of reason for you. My door is always open! Go be great!

To Claudine Caesar, Lynn Graves, Carrisa Jones, the 18 Ivies, the Connector Church, and the MIMS, thank you for being the family that I didn't know that I needed. I thank God for you all. To my Fab 4 sister circle: Dr. Keshia Brown, Dr. Darlene Davis, and Dr. Delores Freeman. It is an honor to have traveled the doctoral journey with you. I'm grateful that our paths crossed, connected, and are now joined forever. We believed that we could, so we did!

I want to extend a special *thank you* to Drs. Diane Wiater and Wes Hall. Dr. Wiater, your mentorship, instruction, and advisement have molded and guided me throughout this leadership experience and transformation. Dr. Hall, thank you for your authentic leadership example, kindness, and willingness to provide your immensely valuable wisdom.

In closing, all praise to my Lord and Savior, Jesus Christ. In Him do I live, move, and have my being. I am truly nothing without You. To God be the Glory!

TABLE OF CONTENTS

FOREWORD

For me, growing up in poverty meant many things, including waiting in line for instructions on what to do. It meant that our voices and input were not solicited, heard, or welcomed. We were to keep our opinions to ourselves. In addition to that, as a child growing up in a Caribbean household, the standard lesson taught by all parents was that *"a child was to be seen, not heard."* These were influences that do not encourage a child to become a leader.

On the other hand, children growing up in more affluent households are generally encouraged to be front and center. They are empowered to challenge the status quo. This was not my reality, which is why I never dreamt that one day people with the best education money can buy would pay attention to my every word as if listening to a well-paid orator. I never imagined that I would be a leader.

One definition of a leader is "the art of motivating a group of people to act towards achieving a common goal." Another is "the person in a group that possesses the combination of personality and leadership traits that makes others want to follow his or her direction." Many leaders are not formally trained and learn to lead through exposure and adversity. Leadership is about embracing challenges and finding solutions rather than avoiding or running away from them. When others witness the way leaders successfully handle problems, they become admirers and turn to that person for guidance. Leadership is not always a naturally occurring quality, and it is challenging to teach. Indeed, management skills are more easily taught, but being a manager and being a leader are two very different traits.

So, what does it mean to be a leader? As a leader, you must be able to assess your team and make whatever adjustments are required. We can learn critical leadership skills by observing the military and sports teams, for example. In both groups, leaders are generally not questioned, even when members of the groups do not fully subscribe to the action plan. The leader can motivate the team to *buy into* the mission, even at times when the task may seem insurmountable.

To create this buy-in, the leader must look at the team and determine who the stars are and create a positive work environment for them. You must also quickly identify people in your organization who do not subscribe to your vision and immediately remove them. Leadership requires the ability to make difficult and uncomfortable choices, but this is the only way to protect your mission, vision, and organizational culture. Managers may be afraid to make such difficult decisions, but leaders are not. Leaders make decisions that work to accomplish the goals of the organization and the people that they lead. They regularly ask themselves, "How can I make my company or my team better?" Once they have the answer, they then make the decisions that are necessary to achieve those outcomes.

Once you have established your team, it is important to have confidence in them. You must allow them the opportunity to be creative. They must have a chance to make mistakes and to learn from them. Team members need to know that they have the respect and appreciation of their leader. A simple "good job" goes a long way and acknowledges their value.

Melva was able to articulate what makes a true leader and ways to help you identify the leadership qualities that will be most impactful. As difficult as it is to lead, it is one of the most rewarding disciplines. Through these pages, which serve as a textbook on leadership, you will explore the trials and rewards of being a leader as well as strategies to identify your personal leadership brand.

Wesley J. Hall

Executive Chairman & Founder

KSS Group of Companies

Honorary Doctorate, University of the West Indies (2017)

Canada's Most Powerful Business People, Canadian Business Magazine (2016)

Vice Chancellor's Award, University of the West Indies (2015)

Ernst & Young Entrepreneur of the Year (2009)

Introduction

GETTING PERSONAL ABOUT LEADERSHIP

"Personal values and influences reflect a silent power that impacts what we are drawn toward and what we are driven away from."[1] –
Watton, Lichtenstein, and Aitken

Leadership is universally recognized as a powerful and critical concept that plays a significant role in achievement and success. Good leadership is noted as the most important competitive advantage of an organization.[2] It generates an influence that ultimately produces impact. Everyone, at some point, has encountered or embodied the qualities of an impactful leader. People want to trust leaders and believe in their visions. They are motivated by competent leaders and inspired to contribute toward the goals and visions those leaders set.

The feelings of impact, influence, motivation, and trust that effective leaders incite do not just occur with every leader. Effective leaders possess a particular makeup of qualities and traits that ignite such specific results. There is a belief and expectation for leaders to guide a movement forward[3] that may have otherwise remained stagnant. The most impactful leaders are those who can identify their qualities and traits and align those appropriately to generate positive outcomes.

The extensive leadership literature of our day focuses on the *what* and *how* of leadership. Numerous definitions, concepts, behaviors, and traits of leadership all aim to pinpoint the "magic formula" that makes leadership effective. However, one vital, yet often overlooked, area lacking in these conversations is the emphasis on the *personal* aspects of leadership.

This book takes a deep dive into the notion of leadership as a personal brand. It provides theories, strategies, examples, and tactics along with evidence suggesting that leadership derives from -- and is influenced by -- a more personal context. I believe that there is no separation between the leader and the person holding the leadership title. Your identity as a leader has a direct correlation to who you are as a person. Your leadership values stem largely from your personal values, and the perceptions of you as a leader are automatically associated with you as an individual.

Accordingly, if leadership output is personal and the results of that output are personal to those influenced by the leader, then one who is considered an impactful leader is so as a result of their personal attributes. The desire and the way that we lead originate from a customized selection of leadership styles, strengths, and approaches that are unique to each person and based on their exposures and influences. No leadership style is identical between different leaders, nor should it be. Leadership is distinctive and should be specific to the leader and leadership environment.

Additionally, how you are viewed as a leader becomes personal because those perceptions represent you. They comprise your brand, and as we will discuss, your brand is your reputation.[4] As we recognize leadership as a personal brand, we will also dissect branding and discuss steps to help you identify who you are as a person and a leader; and how awareness of such qualities contributes to your leadership development, responsibility, and outcomes.

I hope that throughout this book, you will notice ways to incorporate more common leadership concepts with your unique and specific characteristics to create an authentic and influential leadership brand. Let's get started!

Chapter 1

THE MANY FACES OF LEADERSHIP

"Do not follow where the path may lead. Go instead where there is no path and leave a trail." – Unknown Author

Leadership. The *L*-word that is accompanied by hundreds of interpretations and definitions. The topic of leadership has been studied from many different perspectives including traits, behaviors, theories, and styles.[5] The word *leader* will either ignite feelings of gratitude, admiration, and motivation; or conjure up feelings of oppression, distrust, and exploitation. No matter how one defines or relates to the word, it is undeniable that leadership is powerful.

Power represents an essential element of leadership. A leader's power-- the ability to influence-- is an integral dynamic in the correlation between leadership style and leadership outcomes.[6] A leader's use or abuse of power also impacts their reputation and the capacity to be positively influential in achieving goals.

Recognizing the Impact of Your Leadership Brand

There is also a connection between the power holder's actions and their follower's effectiveness, commitment, job satisfaction, effort, and other outcomes.[6] The most effective leaders recognize the responsibility of their power and make intentional efforts to empower others around them. We will discuss this idea more in later chapters but it is important to understand that the use of leadership power is one of several key components of exemplary leadership.

The various approaches to leadership are accompanied by many different leadership styles. These leadership options make it difficult to pinpoint the determinants of what can be considered most effective. As such, leaders must move away from selecting an approach from generic leadership models and use their unique attributes and circumstances to create their own personalized leadership design.

As suggested in the introductory quote, leaders should be trailblazers. They should spark a level of influence that motivates others to follow their responsible[7] leadership path. To reach this level of influence, however leaders must possess certain qualities that begin with an audit of their own personal attributes. Those who are able to merge traditional and personal leadership qualities are positioned to become a positive leadership example. They also become leadership trailblazers with the evolution of their own leadership *brand* that consists of authentic, ethical, and impactful leadership[8] qualities that followers trust.

Think for a moment about your most memorable leader. What traits or characteristics immediately come to mind? For some, you may recall a more positive experience that you had with an outstanding, effective leader. For others, you may immediately think about the "boss-zilla" who was the catalyst for your superior job search skills because every day under his/her leadership, you searched job sites tirelessly looking for ways to *get out quickly!*

Whether positive or negative, I bet that your perception of that person's leadership stems from how he/she made you feel. Their leadership impacted you personally one way or another. You may have thought about their particular leadership style, but I imagine that you also associated the effectiveness or ineffectiveness of that style with how it worked for you. That assessment is common and reasonable. Leaders can ignite feelings of drive, commitment, pride, and excitement. They can also ignite feelings of insecurity, distrust, anxiety, and lack of motivation.

The complicated part about leadership is that although there are numerous leadership theories and behaviors, a leader must determine the specific style(s) that will garner his/her best outcomes. Leaders are torn between two essential concepts: personal and professional leadership. Most leadership discussions center around professional leadership behaviors such as setting a mission, creating a process for achieving goals, aligning processes, and of course, procedures.[9]

Equally as critical however, are personal leadership behaviors. These behaviors include building trust, instilling value, caring for people, and acting morally, in addition to demonstrating skills. The difficult task of the leader is to develop a distinguishable leadership brand that incorporates behaviors from both concepts. These distinguishing factors will be considered when determining your leadership brand in the next few chapters.

So, is there a particular leadership style that is guaranteed to yield the desired results? The short answer is *no*. The only thing concrete about leadership is the desired result: impact. Leadership is an ever-changing, dynamic experience. Nothing will ever be concrete where leadership is concerned. As society changes, technology improves, global interactions increase, and most importantly, people evolve. Leadership styles will also evolve.[10]

Look at how leadership styles have changed so far. Consider the many different methods that currently exist. Leadership styles will expand, theories will continue to evolve, and new approaches will develop; however, one aspect will remain the same. Every leader, no matter the vision, action, or effort, has to build an authentic leadership brand that suits their leadership environment and desired outcomes.

Essentials of Leadership

While there are many styles of leadership, there are some that are beneficial in any circumstance. I believe authentic, transformational, and servant leadership are essential theories that serve as the best foundations for impactful leaders.

Authentic Leadership

Today, there is a desperate need for authentic leaders. Our society is inundated with illusions of reality and deception across many spectrums. We are seeing an alarming increase in the fall of trusted leaders.[11] As a result, the perception and reputation of leadership are changing, and not necessarily for the better. Genuine leaders with creativity, ethics, and confidence are necessary.

Authentic leadership is just that; leadership based on authenticity and honesty.[12] It is a form of necessary differentiation. Authentic leaders:

1. understand their purpose,
2. have strong values about the right thing to do,[13]
3. establish trusting relationships,
4. demonstrate self-discipline,

5. act on their values, and

6. are passionate about their mission.

Authentic leaders possess uniqueness and originality and are not guided by duplicating other models. Establishing an authentic leadership style not only creates a successful leader, but it also helps influence and develop future leaders who will emulate the model provided by genuine leadership examples.

Authentic leaders are different. Just as with fingerprints, authentic leaders are one of a kind. No two authentic leaders are the same because they each have their distinct characteristics and drives that motivate them to do what they do.

When considering the characteristics of your authentic leadership style, think about your own unique qualities. Think about the personal yet positive attributes that you possess:

- Do you have a unique ability to influence?

- Do you have impeccable listening skills that make it easy for others to confide in you?

- Do you relate well with others despite differences?

- Do you incorporate humor into your approach or perhaps compassion?

- Do you know what makes you effective?

The possibilities are endless, but they are your possibilities and comprise elements that distinguish your leadership from others. We will review specific strategies in later chapters that will help you identify and define personal attributes that will enhance your authenticity.

Authentic leaders also thrive off of their sense of purpose.[14] They are usually committed to their mission, and as a result, their passion becomes contagious to those around them. People believe in the authentic leader because they "believe" the authentic leader. Authentic leaders are trustworthy — a personal leadership behavior —and trust is valuable to a follower. It is difficult for an untrustworthy leader to achieve the same level of respect and commitment as one who is well-respected and trusted. Followers appreciate authenticity because it allows the opportunity for a better connection and greater insight.

Consider this example of authentic leadership.

In 2017, French leader Emmanuel Macron made global headlines by defying political odds and securing the win as France's newly elected president. His victory was historic for several reasons. First, President Macron is the youngest French president since Napoleon Bonaparte. Second, President Macron never held a political office before being elected as president. Third, he was never backed by a traditional political party. Although many doubted that such a contradiction of the customary practices would secure a win, President Macron achieved victory with a 66 percent margin. That is a significant achievement.

The French people were generally distrusting of all leaders due to years of political antics. They were ready for someone new and genuine to take the country to the next level.[15] Because of the issues with the previous French leadership, the people of France were determined to try a different approach with a candidate who had a new and authentic approach to politics.[16] As a result, the unexpected victory for the presidency of France went to Emmanuel Macron. Talk about blazing a trail!

Leadership influence is achieved primarily due to the transparency, honesty, and uniqueness that is associated with this particular leadership style. It helps to develop the type of atmosphere that generates loyalty, hard work, and trust. Once others are committed to the leader, the collective impact is dynamic.

Transformational Leadership

The transformational leader is considered a *change agent*.[17] This is a leader who can engage with others and create a connection that ultimately raises the leader's level of influence with those whom he/she connects. A transformational leader makes others feel vital to the team and essential to the overall outcome of the change goal.

The Brand New Leader

When Barak Obama ran for President of the United States in 2008, his election was based primarily on the idea of change. In fact, change was the centerpiece of his campaign. Also, at the forefront of the Obama campaign was a push to connect. What made him so successful during both the 2008 and 2012 campaigns was his ability to connect with American voters. Known as the first social-media president,[18] Obama connected with voters through Facebook, Twitter, events, messaging, and the now-defunct MySpace.

President Obama also made his supporters feel as though they were part of the campaign by using straightforward statements in his messages such as *I need your help;* or, inviting them to *join him* via live streams, chats, or the next big message push. Obama developed an intentional strategy to show supporters that not only did their votes count, but their efforts in the campaign were vital to his success. He made them feel as though he needed them. Their individual efforts, whether big or small, were needed for something as monumental as the election of the next President of the United States.

Supporters became tirelessly involved in organizing social media campaigns, street teams, and other campaign activities. Obama's supporters formed voter registration drives, voter educational and informational sessions, and community engagement activities to keep communities and groups informed of the voting process.[19] Obama's momentum and support increased due to the successful *inclusion* of followers.

Engaging his supporters rather than dictating to them helped his campaign tremendously. Obama successfully secured two terms in office largely because of the relationship that he developed with the American people. His initial slogan, "Yes We Can," made Americans feel as though their fight for a change in politics and government was everyone's fight. They, his voters, felt needed and valued. When followers feel connected to the mission, they are more productive, more committed, and more successful.

Transformational leaders can influence the team to embrace concepts and situations that may otherwise generate resistance. There is a unique ability that these leaders possess to lead through such barriers and potential roadblocks. Transformational leaders make followers feel as though they are part of their solution. They engage with their teams and are attentive to the needs of their followers. Followers feel as though their commitment to the transformational leader also benefits them. The responsibility is not seen as merely one-sided. Followers also see benefits for themselves.

Adopting a transformational leadership model helps the everyday leader build a trustworthy and dependable brand. It also helps build a team that understands its mission and vision due to their connectedness with the leader.

The essential characteristics of transformational leaders include:

1. exhibiting high moral and ethical conduct,

2. motivating followers to reach their highest potential,

3. encouraging and exemplifying creativity and innovative ideas, and

4. providing supportive components to their leadership style for the follower.

Outcomes of a transformational leadership style result in the motivation and empowerment of followers. Additionally, it equips the leader to adapt to other necessary future leadership styles.

Servant Leadership

Servant leadership is primarily associated with religious or nonprofit leadership. However, the qualities of servant leaders are effective across any sector and industry. The servant-leader puts followers and the organizational mission first. This type of leader believes that leadership is about serving. They are self*less* in their motivation to lead while also helping to develop and empower their team.

Throughout the past century, as many leaders and organizations faced tremendous consequences for unethical behavior, servant leaders focused mainly on developing an ethical environment. Of course, as with any leadership style, this is not always the case. However, true servant leaders should find themselves less involved in scandal and more involved in service. By adopting aspects of servant leadership, the followers and the stakeholders are more inclined to feel valued. Servant leaders understand this and are effective because their stakeholders believe in them.

What do servant leaders care about? Well, pretty much everything. They care about their followers, the mission and cause, the stakeholders, and the organization as a whole. Sure, they care about themselves also, but that's not the motivation behind their leadership.

So, let's talk a little about some qualities of a servant leader. The list could go on for a while, but here are the top ten:[20]

1. Listening

2. Empathy

3. Healing and supporting

4. Awareness

5. Persuasion

6. Foresight

7. Generosity

8. Commitment

9. Community Service

10. Stewardship

An excellent example of servant leadership is the late Nelson Mandela. Mr. Mandela, the first black president of South Africa, ascribed to the philosophy that people are empowered by other people and that through unselfish acts, they become their best selves.[21] He is noted for his leadership in the country's transition from apartheid to democracy. His leadership and opposition to an antiapartheid government caused him to experience many struggles. He was sentenced to life in prison for his work to end apartheid.

Throughout the years, Mandela received several offers for freedom if he would renounce the use of violence in efforts to end apartheid. He refused due to his commitment to the cause, even at his own life's expense. Even during his incarceration, his leadership and influence continued. Mandela was able to look beyond the horror of apartheid and the personal injustices he suffered. He did not let his own will, or his individual needs, supersede the will and obligations of the community. That is the essence of servant leadership.

Servant leaders tend to be motivated to empower and build-up something or someone before themselves. They establish trust, build strong relationships, and generate a loyal base of supporters.[22] A common theme of servant leaders is that they are mission-driven and believe in the work of their organization.

The Leadership Concept

Each of the three leadership theories focuses on similar aspects that will help build more reliable connections to both the audience and the followers. They require less focus on individual or personal gain and more of a comprehensive emphasis on the best outcomes for the organization as a whole. Finally, each of the three theories emphasizes the need to stay morally and ethically accountable in order to create and maintain trust.

Every leader must communicate ideas, visions, and messages often and efficiently while working to establish a shared common goal and commitment within the team. A leader must be willing to help grow and develop their team members in addition to providing a creative approach to daily operations. Leadership development that focuses on discovering your most effective and unique leadership qualities will help you customize a leadership style that stands out as capable and trustworthy.

Of course, there are many more leadership styles and even more leadership approaches and traits. The point is to illustrate that there is no cookie-cutter approach to leadership. One size does not fit all, and all leadership methods are not created equally. The theories we've discussed, among others, point to opportunities for evolution. They emphasize a need for learning and, most importantly, customizing new approaches and behaviors as your leadership growth occurs.

Teams are also not created equally. Even within the same team, leaders must understand that each team member is different, and many times, the leadership approach should be adjusted to maximize the potential of that individual. Different teams, employees, and circumstances will require different leadership approaches to achieve the best results.

Thinking back to the leadership styles that have been the most effective or ineffective for you can give you a better idea of how others receive these styles. Going back to our opening question: What traits or characteristics immediately come to mind when you think of your most memorable leader? Why did or didn't their leadership work well for you? How did it make you feel as their follower? Where you more productive and motivated as a result, or were you deflated, insecure, disgruntled, or feeling undervalued? Learning from other leaders (good or bad) and observing the effects of their leadership styles is an appropriate tool. This open-minded perspective provides the opportunity to collaborate and learn from other's experiences. All are vital aspects of growth, productivity, sustainability, and overall leadership success.

Recognizing the Impact of Your Leadership Brand

You may wonder how, given the many definitions and interpretations of leadership, a leader truly filters and develops their own leadership style. How is a leader to be different and distinct when there are hundreds of possible variations of leadership that exist? In the coming chapters, we will explore these ideas and consider a new perspective that ignites more impactful leadership results. We will discuss some foundational theories for leadership development.

Chapter 2

A DIFFERENT KIND OF LEADER

"Leadership begins with the courage to pursue unprecedented actions." -
Melva Robertson

This chapter's quote captures the idea of a different kind of leader, one who is courageous enough to go against the grain and exemplify the qualities of leadership that may be considered uncustomary. In the last chapter, we dissected a few of the more common and positive leadership concepts. Now take the negative connotations and the more stereotypical viewpoints of leadership that you have believed, learned, or heard and (drumroll please), throw those away!

Yes, you heard me correctly. Change your thinking from the more generalized ideas of a leader. Put aside the leadership images of the person with the bullhorn who is leading the pack. Or the idea that a leader is a corporate suit-and-tie-wearing micromanager who sits in an ivory tower looking down upon his lowly subjects. Yes, as difficult as it may be, I want you even to put away the leadership stereotype of the activist and great orator with millions of followers who can single-handedly create a monumental change in history. Sure, they all exemplify a form of leadership; however, they are not leadership standards. Leadership is customized specifically to the leader and comes in the form of any shape, size, industry, or behavior.

These individuals are considered examples of influential leaders in the traditional and well-researched sense. We have heard about the leadership qualities and traits that contributed to their successful outcomes. We understand the nuances that shape these more commonly discussed leaders. Rather than these traditional leaders, consider leaders such as the custodian at the Fortune 500 company. Yes, he/she is also a leader. The sole proprietor with no team who is making a difference through his/her entrepreneurial endeavors is also a leader. The quiet loner who fades into the background yet creates an innovative process adopted by his/her organization is a leader.

As much as it pains me to say, people who mistreat, manipulate, and influence detrimental results are also leaders. Though their circumstances, personalities, positions, or achievements may not rightly illustrate responsible and positive versions of leadership as we know them, they, and others like them, took actions that led to influence. Ultimately, they demonstrated the ability to lead.

Do you know who else is a leader? *You!* The fact that you are reading this book and developing your leadership potential is an indication that there is a leader inside of you just waiting to step forward. Also, I am sure that the leader in you has already emerged whether you realize it or not.

A leader is not always the person at the front of the line. A leader does not always have a large team, nor is there a cookie-cutter approach to leadership. I believe that everyone is a leader at something and at some point. In my opinion, leadership does not begin when someone is following you. As I see it, a *position* is also *not* leadership. An influential and unprecedented action in that moment *is* leadership. I will explain this further in just a moment. Leadership encompasses far more than only a title. I believe that leadership is courageous, innovative, distinctive, influential, and, most of all, leadership is personal.

Many leadership definitions exist partly because leadership is so difficult to define. Nearly 40 years ago, leadership researchers noted that there were almost as many different definitions of leadership as the number of people who attempted to define the concept. There were over 650 leadership definitions at the end of the last century.[23] And, there are many more definitions now and many more to come. I believe that leadership is such a challenge to define because it is personal and specific to each leader. Identifying one's personal nature of leadership offers a better understanding of the specialist knowledge or unique contributions of the individual.[24] Leadership is as distinct as the individual holding the title.

Leadership is transferrable yet ever-changing. For example, a leader who inspires someone else to lead or act transfers that leadership power as they inspire. We talked about this idea earlier when we discussed the leader's -- power holder-- ability to transfer their power through influence. The transference of leadership power does not mean that the qualities of the new leader will be identical to that of the person who inspired it. Inspiring someone to lead or act does not mean that the leadership style or results will be the same. The inspiration behind leadership transference presents differently depending on a particular person, scenario, or need. Though the outcome of leadership is influence, the process through which that outcome is achieved is distinct. Why? Because leadership comes from a personal space, personal exposures, and personal encounters that affect the makeup of one's leadership brand.

The personal aspect of leadership will be discussed more in the next chapter and throughout the book, as we explore the personal leadership brand. Just remember for now that each leader has a leadership brand. One leadership brand will not and should not be identical to someone else's. A leadership brand should represent a compilation of customized leadership qualities, traits, interactions, and styles that represent the leader. Think of this as leadership DNA.

From a corporate perspective, researchers have recognized the leadership brand as a shared identity among an organization's leaders that differentiates what they can do from what rival leaders can do.[25] The premise of the corporate leadership brand is similar to the personal leadership brand in that regard. It looks at the unique qualities that distinguish the leadership styles.

As we explore the idea of a personal leadership brand, the difference is that it provides consideration of the more personal aspects of leadership. The personal leadership brand takes the characteristics of the leadership definition and merges with leadership from a personal branding perspective. It also incorporates nontraditional leaders and their possibly unintentional actions that ignite influence. The personal leadership brand is also a logical response to the increasingly interconnected, globalized, and uncertain business and economic climate that we see today. As additional leadership models emerge, a leadership brand helps the leader remain committed to, and secure in, their leadership identity.

It is important to note that this book defines a leader as *an independent individual who is influential in the forward progression of a process through action.* As we dissect the leadership definition below, notice the personal attributes of the leadership role. It is typically challenging to differentiate the leader from the person because the origin of their leadership style comes from very personal qualities.

An independent individual...

The reference to independence in this definition speaks to the more solitary actions and aspects of leadership. By this definition, an independent leader is one not adhering to a norm or precedent. This type of leader exhibits innovative behaviors. An entrepreneur may fall under the category of *independent*. This person embarks on a journey to create or develop something new and uncustomary. The independent leader does not necessarily follow established guidelines. They possess the courage to explore something different, and as a result of their courageous action, they ignite influence, and in some cases, change.

You may remember the old question, "if your friends jump from a bridge, would you follow them?" In this scenario, and according to leadership definitions, we understand that the *first* friend who jumped from the bridge was the leader. We gather this because the leader influenced the group toward a common goal—subsequently, the others who jumped followed the original leader.

However, according to our perspective of personal leadership, the *independent individual* is the person in the group who decided *not* to follow and ultimately did *not* jump. Why is this person also a leader? Because that person did not follow the norm. The fact that this person acted differently from the standard and courageously created a new option makes that person a leader. Leadership requires the courage to think independently, act, and possess the potential for influence.

...influential

There is that word again: *influential.* Warning! You will see this word often because it is an outcome of the power that leaders hold. Most leadership definitions agree that a leader must ignite influence. I believe that the influence does not have to be intentional. For example, consider the janitor of the Fortune 500 company that we mentioned earlier. This person may work alone, work hard, and work well. He/she may simply smile and say, "have a nice day" to every person with whom he/she encounters.

Having worked in corporate settings before, I can tell you that amid the hustle and bustle of the workday, there are not many smiles, greetings, and salutations. We can imagine that this custodial worker would be engaging in uncustomary practices by speaking and smiling no matter who passes by. Those actions, however, could become contagious and slowly one by one, change the organizational culture because someone could become *influenced* by the actions of the custodian. If this were a real situation, I would classify the custodian as a leader, because though it was happening independently and unintentionally, someone else was influenced by the action.

In a previous role, I was part of a team that worked in silos. Everyone was cordial, but no one took the time to speak, share small talk, or get to know each other. The days were very quiet and focused. We hired a new team member who was the complete opposite of the culture that we'd established. That team member spoke to everyone, stopped in the middle of the day for small talk, and always offered to work collaboratively. Well, without even knowing, that person changed our culture, and in no time, broke down barriers of communication that existed for years. That teammate was a change agent-- a leader. As unintentional as it was, our organizational culture changed with the simple influence of someone who chose not to follow the norm.

...forward progression of a process through action

Forward progression describes the shift that occurs when influence begins to take place. This is usually the moment that someone is recognized as a leader. They may even develop a following at this point. The distinction of this leadership definition is that while leadership is typically defined as an intentional act of influence to a specific group, I believe that an individual is a leader at the onset of their independent action before the forward progression of a process begins.

Leadership occurs when *action* against the norm occurs. The custodian in our hypothetical case became a leader once his/her *actions* of smiling and speaking occurred, not when the *influence* occurred. The action always takes place before the impact. That's the most significant distinction here: leadership, as defined in this book, is action-centered.[26] Leadership is recognized at the onset of action, and action eventually ignites influence.

An entrepreneur becomes a leader once they begin *making* their innovative effort. The team member becomes a leader when they first take the initiative to do something new to progress a process forward. Leadership can occur with anyone, at any time, and with any position. This view of leadership is more inclusive of the various types of leaders that exist.

The broadened leadership definition allows this consideration: the effectiveness of leadership is not determined by good or bad. A "bad" leader is still a leader. These types of leaders have the potential to be just as effective as good ones because their actions still "influence." Leadership effectiveness is determined once the actions of the leader ignite a measure of influence. Whether they have influenced followers to create positive or negative outcomes is a different story that we will discuss in later chapters.

Also, everyone is accountable to someone. Therefore, everyone is a follower. As a result, everyone possesses the ability to influence others for good or bad. One begins to lead when they ignite an *unprecedented* action even if no one is yet following. The leader may not necessarily influence a group; the influence may affect one person or many. Influence also may not immediately occur. Nevertheless, influence is the result of effective leadership actions.

All of this takes courage. It takes courage *not* to follow, to innovate, and to do something different even when there are no followers or support. Courage involves stepping outside the box and taking risks to achieve goals. This is important to remember. Leaders may not initially have a team of supporters, but once the action begins, influence will equate to followers.

Therefore, this book is built upon the idea that everyone has leadership potential; everyone has, at some point led, and everyone has unique leadership qualities that can be developed into an impactful leadership brand. The uncustomary leaders that were described earlier are valuable. They illustrate a fundamental lesson that also resonates throughout this book: leadership is personal and begins with action even before anyone follows. We will explore strategies to develop a leadership brand that generates actions that result in positive and impactful influence.

We will discuss followership later, but the value of the follower for those leaders with teams is another crucial component. Most importantly, as we continue, we will explore strategies and concepts that will help create a distinctive leadership brand. Such a distinction enables leadership that results in positive and impactful influence.

A powerful leadership brand creates quite an impact. Effective leadership can change the world. It can create a lasting imprint that reaches far beyond what even the leader might imagine. Once the personal connection to leadership is recognized as an integral piece of the leadership brand, I believe that we will begin to see an increase in accountability and ethics in leadership.

Chapter 3

UNDERSTANDING BRANDING

"Your personal brand is what people say about you when you are not in the room – remember that. And more importantly, let's discover why!"[27]
– Chris Drucker

Congratulations! It's a brand!

Imagine hearing these words related to the arrival of your brand. You finally understand all of the components over which you once toiled. You know your identity and you have developed your strategy for success. You've labored for quite some time now over every specific detail imaginable concerning your leadership style, your organization, and your tactics to influence. Now you have arrived at the moment when you *deliver* the brand that you've tirelessly worked to conceive.

Hearing "Congratulations! It's a brand," should ignite the same sentiments of love, satisfaction, excitement, and uncertainty that new parents feel when they hear the doctor in the delivery room proclaim, "Congratulations! It's a boy; or, Congratulations! It's a girl!"

The Brand New Leader

In my first book, *Congratulations! It's a Brand: The Entrepreneur's Guide to Birthing the Brand, Increasing Visibility and Identifying Your Target Audience,*" I equate branding to childbirth.[28] The four main stages of childbirth: conception, pregnancy, delivery, and rearing are analogous to what I believe are the four main stages of birthing a brand.

The conception phase is your realization that you want to do this. You know that you want to begin this journey. You may not be completely prepared, but you approach the starting line anyway. During the pregnancy phase, you consume information through research, courses and classes, workshops, degrees, certifications, books, networking, and overall growth focused on understanding everything that contributes to your success.

Next comes delivery. This is the point where you can see the tangible evidence that you are headed in the right direction. You've launched the business, begun the initiative, identified your style, or ignited the effort that you've worked so hard to prepare. When you reach the point of delivery, then comes the hardest part of the entire experience: the rearing phase. This is when you focus on implementing everything that you've learned to ensure the growth and sustainability of the vision your brand represents.

As a leader, whether you lead your own business, product, service, organization, or a cause, you too have become a brand.

Recognizing the Impact of Your Leadership Brand

Your brand has as much impact on the success of your new endeavors as the endeavors themselves. No matter where you are along this journey of leadership discovery, we will start at the beginning and review each of the steps necessary to establish your leadership brand. First things first however: let's make sure that you understand what branding is and involves.

Branding originated as a method to distinguish ownership. Cattle ranchers used hot branding irons to "brand" their identity on cattle so that it was clear which animals belonged to which cattle rancher. The brand was a stamp that was heated in the fire and burned onto the body of the cattle. Ouch! The brand was usually a name or symbol that was unique to that cattle rancher.

In essence, brands were used to identify ownership. Think about it. If there were hundreds of cattle in a field that all looked similar, how would the cattle ranchers know which belonged to whom without these brands? By branding the cattle, there was no mistaking who owned which cattle because each brand was personalized. This is the same concept used today. No matter how many businesses, products, services, or leaders exist, your brand should be identifiable in such a way that makes it undeniably distinguishable.

For example, there are certain restaurants with branded buildings. I don't even mean the reputation or logo; I am referring to actual construction. For instance, the traditional

Pizza Hut building with the red roof is identifiable anywhere. Even if the restaurant no longer operates in that building and the signage has been taken away, it is still recognizable as a former Pizza Hut restaurant. Its identity is distinguishable.

Recently, I was with a friend driving through my childhood neighborhood and sharing a few memories with her. We passed a number of buildings when she said, "I know what that building used to be." Sure enough, she guessed correctly; it was an old McDonald's building. It looked the same as every McDonalds restaurant that any of us have ever seen, even though it had not operated in that capacity in nearly 20 years. The building was now another establishment. In fact, over those years, that building carried many businesses. The McDonald's branding, however, was still distinguishable and undeniable.

Your leadership brand should be just as identifiable. It should uniquely belong to you. As the quote for this chapter mentions, your brand is how others identify you. It's what *they* think of *you* and essentially your identifier among other leaders. Just as hundreds of cattle are unmistakably identifiable to their various owners, there will be other businesses, titles, products, and people with similar ventures and goals as yours. What makes you stand out and identifiable amongst them is your leadership brand identity.

Recognizing the Impact of Your Leadership Brand

Consider this; there are billions of people in this world, but no two people are exactly the same. Notice I didn't say similar; I said exactly the same. Even identical twins or other multiples have unique features and factors that distinguish them. There is always a distinguishing factor that helps you know the identity of everyone on this planet. Of course, all people have the same standard features. Generally speaking, everyone structurally is composed the same way. Yet differentiating factors characterize the unique identity of each person.

When I visit my daughter's classroom at school, I walk in and see about 15 human beings; but each one is distinguishable even though they may look similar in some regard.

Let's look at the differences. First, they are either boys or girls. Then, with the boys, although they wear uniforms and have on the same clothes, they may wear their clothes differently. Some boys are smaller than others; some have different complexions, different ethnicities, or their voices sound different. The same is true with the girls. Some have blue eyes, while others may have brown or hazel eyes. Some of the girls have shorter hair than others while they all have different body types.

Of all the children, some have braces, glasses, curly hair, or straight hair. They all have different personalities that are also distinguishable. I'm sure that at the beginning of the year, their teachers had to concentrate on these differences in order to distinguish each child from the other. But, in a short time, those differences were helpful in identifying one another. That distinguishable factor is equivalent to their brand. It's their identity. Even at those young ages, everyone is distinguished by some aspect of their identity.

This is an opportunity to pause for just a moment and note that the same scenario applies to your leadership brand. There will be plenty of similarities between yours and other brands. Just as mentioned earlier, no two brands are the same. As long as your brand is unique and specifically true to your qualities, strengths, and values, there will always be a difference.

Understanding branding is necessary for determining your own leadership brand identity and strategy. Typically, when thinking about a brand, there is an automatic association with a product or business; and that's not necessarily wrong. It's not entirely correct either. Branding has become one of those words that has taken on various meanings. Throughout my career, I've heard clients refer to branding in every way from their website, business cards, a logo, a product, their business name; the list goes on. In reality, all of these components are connected to branding, but when thinking about the branding definition, there are two main possibilities.

The first definition of branding refers to what is called the brand name—usually of a product or service. This definition focuses more on the name and visually distinguishing factors of the product. We can think of a brand name as synonymous with a trademark. For instance, Disney is a brand name. Everything that falls under the Disney umbrella – theme parks all over the world, movies, cruises, television channels, merchandise, characters, radio, and so many other facets -- connects to the Disney brand name. What also happens when we refer to a brand name is that everything associated with that brand name must align with that brand. I'll talk more about that in a moment, but generally speaking, if Disney is the brand name, then everything associated with it will match Disney's reputation.

Another well-known brand name is Apple. In fact, Apple was deemed one of the most successful *brands* of our generation.[29] The Apple brand name includes many products such as the iPad, computers, music, phones, and, under each of those products, there are several other products. Apple's success depends largely on its very specific strategy, detail, and attention to its brand. There is particular attention to the Apple brand--not just brand name-- because they have a set of brand alignment strategies from which they do not deviate. This means that no matter what Apple products you encounter, it has a very unique, yet simple, Apple identity.

Branding, as defined in this book, is a reputation or identity. It's the attributes of the brand name or trademark.

Whether referring to a business, consumer, corporate, or personal brand, the concept is how people characterize that entity, that brand. The brand outlines what is valuable and most distinct. An effective brand's delivery aligns with what people perceive.[30] The branding definition shifted around the late 20th century when marketing professionals realized that the impression left from a product was more impactful than just the name and look of that product.

People will always remember a feeling. Mormon leader Carl Buehner once said, "People may forget what you said, but they will never forget how you made them feel."[31] This captures the strategy behind branding. The goal is to create a positive feeling and lasting impression on your followers. A brand is now identified as the feelings and attributes evoked when others think of a product, service, organization, or *you*.[32]

Think about it this way: we all want to evoke certain feelings when people hear our name and think of us. Usually, we want those feelings and identifying attributes to be positive ones. For example, the guy from your high school class who was always outgoing, telling jokes, and making people laugh probably wanted to be identified as the funny guy. His brand was perhaps *class clown* or something that spoke to his ability to make people happy. The high- achieving student who always made the honor roll and received numerous achievements and awards for academic abilities would probably want his/her brand to involve intellectual success and achievements. This would more than likely be the same person who was voted most likely to succeed. Both reputations were based on the energy and qualities and outcomes that the individuals presented to their various audiences. How they were perceived aligned well with what they delivered.

The other important piece to this branding puzzle is that intention is not reality. Just because you *want* someone to consider your brand in a certain way, does not mean that others will receive your brand that way. In other words, "you get out what you put in." This is why branding is such an important topic. It requires tenacity and proactive strategy to deliver what you indicate you will deliver.

Companies can tout that they are the best or that they have a particular type of service or quality. But if their actions do not align with that message, their audiences will develop their perceptions of the company, which essentially becomes the company's brand identity. The company with the reputation of less than stellar customer service that boasts of quality customer service has not achieved brand alignment because what they promised to deliver is not what their customers received.

Let's take another trip back to high school for a moment. Those students who were always in trouble, or were bullies, may not have wanted their reputations to be negative. Yet because of their actions, the teachers, students, and administrators had their own thoughts of the brand.

I come from a family of educators, and throughout my life, I can recall family members mentioning their students with "bad brands." The reputations of these students preceded them and also lasted far beyond their tenure at the school. There are conversations even today from former educators that, when reminiscing about former students, immediately recall student encounters — positive and negative — that haven't occurred in years. Why? Because the student left a lasting impression and the educators vividly remember how those students made them feel.

Think about this for a moment: what are some adjectives that you think people attribute to you? Do you feel that others are receiving your actions in the way in which you intended?

As we think about the top brands from earlier, what do you think makes those brands most identifiable? Is it their brand name, or is it the impression that they leave with their audiences? My answer is that it is the impression. Disney and Apple can deliver the products and services that they promised in the way they promised. As a result, they have successful brands because they are able to deliver consistently; and that delivery leaves a lasting impression.

Recognizing the Impact of Your Leadership Brand

When thinking about Disney, we usually think of happiness and the beloved *Disney magic*. That was the intention of the company from its first beginning days with founder Walt Disney. Mr. Disney wanted to create happiness through magical experiences. Everything that you encounter that is associated with Disney conveys joy and majesty. Developing a brand is easier when you are clear on what you want to convey and how you want people to feel. Then you should work strategically to achieve those goals at every opportunity.

Apple is known for its high-end products, quality, simple yet innovative designs and features. Apple's audience is not expecting the next *iWhatever* that comes out to be low cost or low quality because that is not what that brand has communicated. The audience knows that, along with the price tag, comes a quality product. They know this from encountering the Apple experience; it's what the company aims to prove. As a result, every two years or sooner, when Apple launches the next big product, consumers are anxious to purchase.

Brand alignment is what successful brands like Disney and Apple are able to achieve. They have mastered the art of delivering on the results and expectations that they have promised in a consistent and highly distinguishable manner.[33] What they communicate about their brands aligns with how the public perceives and interprets their brands.

Did you notice that I said, *continues* to prove? Consistency is also a huge factor in establishing an effective brand.[34] You have to be consistent with the messages that you transmit to the public and you must be consistent with the delivery of your promises. If not, your brand will quickly become associated with whatever the most consistent message is that you deliver — whether positive or negative. Companies known for negative customer service garnered that reputation because they consistently demonstrated those attributes. They left a negative impression when interacting with customers.

In contrast, companies with superior customer service, clean facilities, quality products, or effective leadership earn that brand designation because they consistently work to ensure that they are living up to the reputation that they desire. They work intentionally to leave a positive, lasting impression. Your brand communicates the value that you have to offer[35] -- whether intentional or not.

Now let's take this a step further. Branding does not just apply to a business or product. As I mentioned before, there is also what's known as the personal brand. We have somewhat discussed this throughout the chapter as we've talked about the reputations of individuals, but personal branding is also a key concept in the professional world. A personal brand is your public persona that stands for something clear and influential that your audience attributes to you.[36]

Recognizing the Impact of Your Leadership Brand

Brands are powerful and effective largely because they evoke personal feelings. Most brand-influenced decisions are made based on trust, confidence, and the connection that we feel about a brand.[37] People believe in your brand based on their feelings. Branding is also effective at influencing others because it's the most compelling method of influence. This is due to the connectivity aspect of branding.

Think back to the personal leadership behaviors such as building trust, caring for people, acting morally, that we discussed in Chapter 1. These behaviors connect to how others feel about your brand. Those feelings, more so than your promises, are what define your reputation and the perceptions of you as a leader. The feelings that brands evoke result in decisions made based on the connection between feelings and the brand. Therefore, branding is vital to effective leadership because a considerable measure of leadership success is based on the ability to influence and create trust effectively. Everything about branding is personal which is why there is such a strong connection to leadership and personal branding.

Let me give you the best example of a dynamic personal brand: Oprah. Oprah Winfrey's personal brand is so clear and influential that we don't even need her last name. The brand that she developed for herself plays a large part in her success and sustainability throughout the years.

But what makes her brand this way? It's the fact that throughout her career, she provides the public with a consistent persona that delivers quality, sensibility, results, and excellence across all of her endeavors. More so, Oprah demonstrates authenticity and sincerity in who she claims to be. If you scan the course of her career, Oprah remains consistent in the essence of who she is. Her name and platform have evolved largely due to her strong sense of brand awareness and understanding of the image that she wants to portray.

The personal brand is your method of delivering *you* to the public in the most strategic and well-composed way. It represents your values, skills, qualities, and unique attributes that distinguish you from others. Creating your personal brand is sometimes challenging, but necessary. It requires an understanding of who you are and what you want people to feel and achieve when they encounter you.[38] When you find that others perceive your brand the way that you intend for them to, then you have discovered your brand and achieved brand alignment.

The Leadership Factor

The next thing for us to think about related to personal branding is the leadership factor. If you are reading this book, then you most likely consider yourself a leader. What I want you to realize however, is the connection between you as a leader and you as a personal brand. It is personal. Just as with every other aspect of branding that we've discussed, your leadership brand conveys your identity and your distinction as a leader.[39] The leadership brand is also the driving force behind your effectiveness as a leader. Combining the leadership influence with the branding influence potential creates quite an impactful dynamic. It is also necessary that your leadership brand communicates who you are as a leader. You, as a leader, become associated with *you* as a person and vice versa. There is no distinction.

Assuming a leadership role is an enormous responsibility. Many aspire to lead and possess the qualities to do so. However, having the title or job skills is not what makes one a leader. Leadership is about impact; merely holding a leadership title is just not enough. Your leadership brand must encompass the attributes that garner the trust, confidence, and value that your audience expects to receive.

How you represent yourself, your strengths, values, and delivery are all essential elements in your leadership brand. The same rationale for the need to establish any brand also applies to leadership branding. Leadership branding has become more valuable and impactful than even corporate branding in most cases. This is because it is easier to trust people than companies;[40] and people are also better to interact with and are more accountable to their brand promises.

The Brand New Leader

Your leadership brand helps you recognize, identify, and commit to your leadership style. You may already have what you feel is an effective leadership brand, but is it the right brand for what you are trying to accomplish? Does your leadership brand create the best results for your team? Are you achieving the best outcomes from your team and your audience? The wrong leadership brand for your goals will not yield your desired results. If your brand isn't intentional, it is easier to get distracted and deviate from your desired goals. Your brand helps you align your priorities within the beneficial opportunities available and the tasks that you will undertake.

Leadership branding represents your values. As you build your leadership brand it will become an honest reflection of yourself whether you want it to or not. This is partly the reason that leadership branding is so personal. A brand that is true to who you are will become a brand distinctive of you. I am referring to a brand that is true to the genuine nature of you as a leader. This brand is based on your desires, motivations, and the essence of who you are.

Later chapters dive deeper into the steps to establishing your leadership brand. Meanwhile, as you think more about your leadership brand, consider this question: What do you want to be known for as a leader?

Chapter 4

THE RESPONSIBILITIES OF A LEADER

"Leadership is accompanied by overwhelming responsibility, power, pressure, and, most importantly, accountability to many." – Melva Robertson

Previously I asked how you want others to view your leadership brand. To answer, I would like to revisit the questions that I posed at the beginning of this book. What comes to mind when you think of leaders? Do you think of effective leaders and their positive leadership attributes, or do you think of the more negative experiences that you've had with weak leaders?

Now, let's expand these questions a bit more. The first question: in which category of leadership do you think you fall? My follow-up question is this: what are the characteristics that you exhibit that justify the category that you've placed yourself into? If you consider yourself an honest leader, what have you done or not done to demonstrate that honesty? Do your two responses align? Whether they do or not, this next discussion will help you improve in areas that reflect a positive, effective, and influential leadership brand.

The Brand New Leader

As you think about the types of leaders that you've encountered, are you associating each type with positive, warm, and fuzzy feelings, or is it something less than stellar? The way you feel about, or how you identify with a brand, speaks volumes about their impact. The same goes for your brand. How people associate your brand is directly related to your level of influence and thus, your effectiveness.

No matter what one thinks of leaders, the feelings more than likely connect to something personal. Whether effective or ineffective, the influence is based on how the leader made you feel. Were you inspired to do more? Where you lacking in self-confidence? Were you motivated to create new initiatives? Either way, the leader's actions caused you to react accordingly.

Given the impact of leadership on each of us, it makes sense that leadership is a brand. Yet, the leadership brand itself has diminished over time. Given the number of ineffective leaders throughout history and their disregard for the enormous responsibility placed on leaders, the leadership brand reputation has suffered.

Unfortunately, events across the decades reflect a consistent pattern of leadership blunders that have contributed to the public's distrust of leaders. Leadership guru Peter Northouse attributes this distrust to the many scandals that have led to the increased skepticism of those in authority. Although we hear a lot about corporations, it is not solely corporate leaders who have these mishaps. Unfortunately, leaders in non-profit, government, religious, and so many organizations are facing the consequences of their irresponsibility. Rather than inciting feelings of value, trust, and confidence from their teams, the abuse of power ignites feelings of helplessness, inequity, frustration, and distrust.

History is filled with examples of unethical leadership, such as President Richard Nixon's infamous Watergate scandal that exposed his administration's dishonest reelection tactics. Or, the energy-trading company Enron's fraudulent reporting of their revenue, which impacted thousands of employees and investors. Celebrities within our popular culture and other known leaders have also demonstrated unethical leadership and self-serving actions.

Even religious leaders have demonstrated unethical behaviors, infidelity, financial fraud, and manipulation. The Roman Catholic Church experienced years of a tarnished reputation for the growing cases of sexual misconduct. Pastors are scrutinized for various leadership mishaps, government leaders around the world have chosen poorly thought-out or misguided options that have negatively impacted the lives of people who depend on and trust them.

Similar cases of non-ethical leadership values are also prevalent in the non-profit, academic, and business sectors. These industries are also vulnerable to issues of misappropriation of funds, embezzlement, and much more. Succumbing to the temptation of abusing authority is possible for any leader regardless of their industry or sector. Leaders must be aware of and vigilant about ways to avoid such happenings. They should also be aware and in tune with how others react to their leadership style.

These types of leadership crises are not new. The debate surrounding leadership character has carried on for centuries. From the time of the early church to the present day, there is a sense of desperation for more leaders who exemplify strong character, ethics, and deeply held values. Along with the more evident and tangible outcomes of an effective leader, ethics, humanity, and honesty are all aspects of leadership that are just as impactful as a clear and concise vision, well-developed strategy, and business know-how. The leadership role is more than power, skill, and prestige.

As mentioned at the beginning of this chapter, leadership is accompanied by overwhelming responsibility and pressure. Responsibility is most often synonymous with accountability and dependability for performance; and the ability to *act* appropriately. Although the idea of *appropriate* is subjective, it associates responsible actions with doing good and promoting good. One definition of a capable leader is one who builds and sustains social and moral relationships between the leader and followers based on a sense of justice, recognition, care, and accountability for a wide range of economic, ecological, social, political, and human responsibilities.

Leadership is a role that should not be taken lightly but taken with detail and intent. We must cover leadership responsibility and accountability because a way to ruin your leadership brand is to fall victim to the traps and temptations that have caused so many others to fail.

Despite these cases of improprieties however, there are proven role models for ethical and moral leaders who understand the responsibility associated with their roles. The world is filled with exemplary leaders who have accomplished remarkable achievements and blazed trails for others behind them. Unfortunately, as the saying goes, "one bad apple spoils the bunch." Solidifying an intentional, positive, and ethical brand will help shift the leadership narrative to a more positive tone.

Although there are likely more ethical and effective leaders than there are immoral and unethical ones, the consistently negative coverage and publicity that the *bad apples* receive suggests the opposite. Because of this, good leaders face an even larger responsibility to help restore and defend the honor of the leadership role. These leaders are charged to rebuild and redefine the leadership brand. That is such a high level of responsibility, however as noted previously, to whom much is given, much is required.[41] After all, as a leader, you are inherently built to take on seemingly impossible or challenging tasks. That is why you are the leader.

Positive leadership begins and ends with ethical leadership that operates with integrity. Remember, leadership effectiveness is not determined by good or bad but by the ability to influence. One measurement of good or bad leadership however, is determined by ethical behavior. Due to the growing leadership concerns of our time, the training and preparation of all leaders must include a realignment to ethical leadership; ultimately creating leadership brand alignment. People want to believe that leaders are who they portray themselves to be.

As we've discussed previously, brand alignment takes place when your idea of your brand's image aligns with other's perceptions of your brand. Leadership branding involves specific competencies that are targeted to meet the leadership needs that are lacking in the present day.

A solid, exemplary leader gains the trust of the followers and stakeholders and reshapes the perception of leadership. Additionally, if these types of leaders lead by example, they are also setting a new model for future leaders. Remember, leaders can be both positive and negative influences. Yes, the leadership role is a challenging one; but those challenges should not have to manifest into yielding to desperate acts that tarnish the reputation of both the leader and the organization.

Recognizing the Impact of Your Leadership Brand

Leaders must embark on their leadership journey with a realistic understanding of the responsibility that they hold. To establish an ethical leadership brand, everything is at stake for each decision or action that leaders make. This means certain leadership qualities cannot be ignored when developing as a leader.

When thinking of leadership, there are several considerations. Let's explore a few that research shows are the more prominent aspects of leadership. Our exploration will emphasize why this role involves such a high level of responsibility.

Leadership is an honorable position.[42] There was a time when the position of the leader was respected -- within any context. Regardless of the situation, the position of authority that was considered *leader* was highly respected and cherished.

Consider the office of the President of the United States. The United States has elected 46 presidents, and I am confident that no sitting president has been liked, endorsed, or supported by every single American during their term in office. It is not realistic to believe that everyone will support their leader, any leader, or that they agree that the person in that position is the best option. However, one thing that remains clear is that the majority of US citizens recognize the value and the honor associated with the office of President of the United States. We know this because US voter turnout among eligible voters during presidential elections averages roughly 60 percent.[43] Midterm elections average roughly 40 percent of voter turnout with local and primary elections falling even lower.[44]

These statistics demonstrate that whether or not people agree with the person elected, they do understand the significance and potential impact of that role and the potential implications of having the right (or wrong) person in the office. Think about this; our past presidents are not categorized collectively when it comes to their leadership styles, or whether they were "good or bad leaders." They are based solely on their individual, personal record of leadership.

People look at the leadership role in much the same way. They understand that the leadership position is filled by the person who will help facilitate the most significant impact for that entity. Even when trust or respect for the leader is lacking, there is still hope for the role. When a leader breaks the confidence of the team, that individual is replaced, but the position remains. This goes back to the idea of leadership as a personal brand. Leaders are judged individually based on their personal leadership brand.

As a leader, it is important to understand the honor of a leadership position because it puts into better perspective its value and prominence. Hopefully, when a leader understands the true value, expectation, and responsibility that they hold, they accept that responsibility with care and treasure it as if it were a precious, invaluable gift. This point of view guides their actions and can lead to a new leadership brand.

Leadership Quality. Can leaders afford to make mistakes? Absolutely. Can leaders afford to be irresponsible, careless, or unethical? Absolutely not. Understand that there is a difference between making a business blunder and leading the company into a corporate scandal. A wrong business decision is generally experiencing a different outcome than expected for a particular business strategy. Companies regularly experience situations where a campaign didn't produce the expected outcomes. Although there are times where the repercussions can call for more strategic methods to achieve an appropriate resolution, it is not the same as corruption. One fitting example of a good idea gone wrong is the disastrous "Pay Your Age" promotion by Build-A-Bear Workshops.

Anyone with a toddler or young child is probably familiar with Build-A-Bear Workshops. If you are like me, you cannot walk through the mall with your child, pass by a Build-A-Bear store and not be bombarded with several, "Please! Please! Please! Can we go in?" requests. This is the store that takes kids on an interactive journey to bring their customized stuffed animal to life. Children pick the animal that they want, groom it, give it a heart, stuff it themselves, and "Voila!" the bear is theirs' for the taking... to the cost of approximately $50 or more after you've purchased clothes and accessories.

Given the popularity and hefty price tag, it's no wonder that kids and parents (both for different reasons), went into a frenzy at the opportunity to only pay their child's age to build a bear. If you had a two-year-old, your price was $2 for a bear. The one-day campaign went out to a members-only list and boasted of the opportunity.

On the day of the promotion, I'm sure the outcome was not what leadership expected. Long lines of patrons crowded stores and malls. Most stores ran out of inventory very early on. Fights erupted between hostile parents, toddlers cried, and hours were wasted by parents and kids who stood in line only to be turned away without merchandise because all stores closed early. This plan did not go over well and leadership ended up issuing many apologies and vouchers to lots of disgruntled parents with unhappy and disappointed children.

While it is true that Build-a-Bear felt the residual fallout of that experience, it was just a poorly executed plan that leaders did not thoroughly consider. Did the campaign have adverse outcomes? Yes; but that is entirely different from corporate scandal, lies, allegations, manipulation, and federal investigations. There is a difference; and while leaders are not expected to be perfect, they should be trustworthy and ethical.

Leaders must take intentional actions toward building the trust of all stakeholders. Due to the questionable character of past leaders, a leadership reestablishment is necessary.

Recognizing the Impact of Your Leadership Brand

Leadership development tactics need a strong emphasis on ways to resist and avoid potentially disastrous situations and practices. While the office of the leader is respected, the individual(s) holding that office should do so without causing disgrace and shame to themselves or others. Leaders should have a strong enough character and will to remain trustworthy. Your leadership brand depends on your ethical character.

Leaders don't have personal lives. This statement may raise a few objections. You are probably saying, "What do you mean, 'leaders don't have personal lives?'" To an extent that's a very true statement although not as black and white as it may seem. Similar to celebrities, leaders of any group are under higher scrutiny and closer observation. This is especially true for your leadership brand because your leadership brand is, as we discussed, a personal brand. It communicates personal values, personality, vision, and abilities to the appropriate audiences to generate a positive emotional response.[45] Your profile is everyone's business and interest. Having a positive professional reputation is rapidly becoming a necessity for personal and corporate success. It is what your brand is built upon.

Given the high level of scrutiny leaders experience, does character matter for leaders? Some will say yes, and others will disagree. My recommendation, however, is to allow values, ethics, and morals to guide all personal and professional leadership decision-making so that you won't have to find out whether it matters or not. Private indiscretions are never private; which is why I started this section with the fact that leaders don't have private lives. When personal and professional misdeeds become public, there are so many other variables that are affected.

For instance, consider the leader exposed for their private indiscretions. That exposure not only affects the leader, but there are also implications to the organization, the team, and the leader's family and loved ones. We often see leaders fired and ridiculed for making comments on their own social media pages, or for domestic situations within their own private lives. That's their personal time though correct? Wrong. Your actions affect your brand. If they did not, then we would not see such disassociation by others when negative actions take place. Disassociation happens because other brands don't want to be impacted by a negative brand and potentially divisive behavior.

We see this often with celebrities-- who some may or may not agree are leaders. Regardless of your stance on that, celebrities are influential public figures. In fact, advertisers have analytics that suggest that the average person is more likely to purchase a product or, at least consider a product, if their favorite celeb endorses it. This is the main reason companies pay celebrities, or-- as they call them on social media-- influencers, large amounts of money to endorse a product. It is also the reason that these same companies fire those celebrities with tarnished personal brands.

That is influence. I've seen leadership definitions that describe the ability to influence a group as a quality of leadership. So, when these public figures make mistakes, their mistake becomes the top news story and social media trends because once again, another trusted source has broken the trust of their followers. This is even the case when the indiscretions solely pertain to the public figure's private life. Fair or not, there is an expectation placed on leaders and persons of influence that cannot be taken for granted. When considered a leader, there is a responsibility and accountability that cannot be overlooked. Leaders must understand the level of responsibility associated with their brands.

So, what's a leader to do? I'm glad that you asked. I have the answer for you in the next chapter as we explore specific tools and strategies to help you remain an accountable and ethical leadership brand.

Chapter 5

TOOLS FOR AN ETHICAL LEADERSHIP BRAND

"Remember, leadership is an action – your action. Your leadership brand and actions convey your identity." – Melva Robertson

To garner a positive leadership brand that is well-respected, exemplary, and successful, your reputation through your actions must align with such qualities. In this chapter, we look at tools that are helpful for all leaders. These tools help strengthen the possibility of withstanding the extraordinarily tempting and potentially dangerous leadership cultures that have developed over the years. One note of reassurance is that there are plenty of excellent leaders before us, who have provided a useful model for establishing and maintaining desirable leadership brands. Let's discuss these leaders and some other valuable tools that will yield our desired results.

Recognizing Your Brand. Recognizing and acting as though your leadership style is a personal brand helps strengthen your level of accountability.[46] If you think of leadership as something you do that affects your business, there is a separation that detaches you, the leader, from the effects and possibility of potential consequences. However, when you recognize that leadership is not a role per se, but essentially it is you with no separation or detachment, most will *act* a bit more cautiously.

Leadership is an action — your action. Your leadership brand and actions convey your identity. How people think of you as a leader is also a part of who you are. How people associate you as a person to your leadership should cause you to take more ownership and accountability as a leader because it is personal. Reshaping your understanding of these concepts helps you identify your leadership from a more personal context.

Ethical Leadership. Ethical leadership requires accountability. Considering the amount of responsibility, accountability, and judgment of leadership outcomes and decision-making, having sound guidance is an excellent way to relieve some of the leadership pressures. Mentorship is a way to aid leaders in growth and development. A mentor is equally as necessary for gaining counsel and fulfilling the challenge to become better.[47]

Further, mentorship is similar to the checks and balances process, with more guidance added. Mentorship helps leaders make informed, rather than emotional decisions.[48] Relying on mentorship, accountability, and accepting the responsibility of the leadership role, helps reduce the chances of leadership blunders.

Thoughtful Decision-Making. Along with recognizing leadership as a personal brand and finding guidance through a mentor, thoughtful decision making is another component of being an ethical leader. Leadership decision-making has a long-lasting and far-reaching impact (both good and bad). Ultimately, the implications of the decisions made, fall on the leader. Even in uncomfortable situations, leaders must make the right decisions. The boldness to make the *right* decision is a true testament of leadership in itself. We've talked about leadership courage and making an unprecedented decision as one of the more courageous requirements of leaders. The first step in decision-making is to think about the potential effects of those decisions and who will be impacted the most.

I often wonder if leaders who are exposed for scandal ever considered the possibility of the backlash that could result. Hindsight is 20/20, but if leaders could foresee the repercussions of their choices before making them, would they make better decisions? If we know that our decisions would result in imprisonment, or a highly publicized judicial process, the loss of my family, or a permanently tarnished reputation, hopefully, we would choose the option that does *not* yield those types of results. I believe that many times individuals making disappointing ethical decisions are sure that they will not get caught, they do not consider the repercussions, or they have ethical blindspots[49] that we will discuss shortly.

The thoughtful decision-making process is a time to weigh the pros and cons seriously. It may even be wise to go ahead and assume that you will "get caught" and then consider if those consequences would be worth experiencing. We are speaking specifically about ethics I know but thinking before you act is a good practice in general. Usually, when we second-guess ethics-based decisions, it is because the answer will be *no, it's not worth it.*

Remember being a kid and your friends tried convincing you to do something that you know your parents would disapprove of? Or, maybe you were the friend or sibling doing the convincing; after all, you are now a leader and leaders are skilled influencers, right!? Either way, one of the justifications used to convince the others to go ahead and commit the offense was always, "you won't get caught!"

But you did get caught! Immediately after your parents found out, there was probably regret on your part. Usually, in my case anyway, during the punishment, I found myself wishing that I never committed the offense. It just didn't feel worth it anymore. The remorse felt after getting "caught," usually causes regret. Even if you are only remorseful at the fact that you "got caught," it still ends up not being worth it. Thoughtful decision-making allows you to take the time to think about those consequences and the *what-ifs*. Doing so should convince you that the wrong option is not the right decision. Remember, leaders do not have personal lives because there is no distinction between the leader and the person.

The Accountability Model

We have talked about the need for mentorship and effective decision-making. This thoughtful strategy for maintaining a positive leadership brand makes up what I refer to as an accountability model. Leaders need ethical competence, which is the ability of a decision-maker to use the right way to think, in front of a moral problem. The accountability model is a checklist of sorts that helps you remain on track in the steps to remain ethical. Your accountability model includes aspects such as establishing and conferring with your mentor, thinking through various scenarios to help you make informed decisions that speak to your integrity, and establishing and implementing your ethical leadership model. The factors that you set within your accountability model aid in ensuring that you have and utilize your customized tools to remain responsible.

A leader's behavior, leadership, and actions in general, should be guided by something. It is quite possible that leaders do not even recognize their actions as inappropriate and surrender to the many pressures that accompany the leadership position. This is why it is so crucial that ethical and accountable leaders possess integrity above all else.

Some believe that a person's integrity helps shape their ethical lens while others see ethics and integrity as interchangeable. Let me pose this question to you. In your opinion, which comes first, integrity or ethics? Ethical behavior is an *act* of integrity.[50] Integrity is also the foundation for all decision-making. Let's explore ways to ensure leadership integrity.

The Code of Ethics

While some ethical decisions require insight and sound judgment, others are not as absolute and involve a much more significant consideration of ethical norms. These are baseline codes of ethics or the standard behaviors that represent an organizational or societal stance. Consider these as ethical norms, or guidance on acceptable practices for your brand. Identifying these norms is useful for accountable leaders and also beneficial for those leaders who need to boost their ethical gauge when making difficult decisions.

A large body of research exists that includes models to prevent unethical leadership behaviors. This consists of the need to improve the compliance of ethical standards. The solution sounds simple; leaders must do the right thing. The problem is—and this is where we look at ethics—there is not always a standard consensus of what the *right* action entails. It is all relative.

Ethics is a collection of what can be considered normal behaviors by which people agree to operate.[51] Although this concept seems clear, the application of it is not as straight-forward. Any leader can fall subject to ethical blindspots—these are actions that leaders do not recognize as unethical. A small example of an ethical blindspot may consist of a leader accepting a gift from a vendor of the company that bids for the company's business. Some consider this a simple "thank you" perhaps for recent transactions, while others view it as an unethical practice because it seems like bribery.

The lines can easily become blurred in some cases. Leaders do not always recognize the ethical dimensions of their decisions because they are subject to those ethical blindspots; and some of the scenarios are subjective.[52] Most unethical behaviors stem from actions that individuals don't see as unethical. Both blatantly unethical tactics, as well as ethical blind spots, have led to good leaders crossing ethical boundaries. This is why standards and guidelines help determine your ethical standards as a leader. These standards help gauge when such situations may become blurred.

As a leader, it is very necessary to consider all possible ethical blindspots in a situation *and* how specific actions can also result in ethical blindspots for the follower. That's where the thoughtful decision-making that we discussed earlier comes into play. Leaders have to consider all possible alternatives in every situation before making decisions, especially decisions that may seem questionable. When thoughtful decision-making does not occur, everyone suffers. Whether intentional or not, everyone is impacted by a business scandal or corruption allegation.

Let me give you an example. In 2015 there was a conviction of 12 educators and administrators of the Atlanta Public School System in Atlanta, Georgia. This very high-profile case involved some staff within the school system changing and affecting the results of standardized test scores. These acts were allegedly a directive from the central office. Thousands of students were affected by the decade-long cheating scandal. According to 2011 reports from the Office of the Governor of Georgia's Special Investigators team, "teachers and administrators gave children answers, erased incorrect answers, hid and altered documents, offered monetary incentives to encourage cheating and punished employees who refused to cheat." This case involved more than 178 administrators and teachers from 44 elementary and middle schools within the school system.

Now that you have the background, here is my point. This was a widely publicized scandal that affected a lot of people ranging from students to parents, the school system, communities, city and state, and educators and their families. Yes, some were aware that what they were doing was blatantly unethical. I would imagine that the senior leaders were the most conscious, but what about the educators and staff members who were just *doing their jobs?* Consider those who were involved indirectly, not knowing that their actions were part of a larger federal crime. According to reports, some educators received backlash and reprimands for not adhering to what was an unethical norm.

We understand that cheating itself is unethical, but what about unknowingly reporting the *new* scores, or following the directions and examples of your leader under an organizational mandate, or, from the pressure of losing your job for not following directions. I would imagine that there were several ethical blindspots for some not closely connected to the inner workings of the senior leadership. However, nearly everyone in the school system was involved and most certainly impacted in some capacity.

This scenario points right back to the responsibility of a leader. This scandal began at the top, and the trickle-down effect was enormous. Educators and their families, parents, children, the school system as a whole were all affected by one decision that was either initiated or allowed by the person held responsible for the organization—the leader. How, then, can leaders remain ethical if they do not always recognize negligence in their leadership actions? A model necessary to rectify this issue exists and can be used to help leaders remain as esteemed as the leadership role itself. Leaders must always be aware of potential pitfalls. I view the precautions that leaders must take as the same precautions a person would take stepping into a field of landmines. One wrong move and *boom!* You may step on an *abuse of power* explosive, an *ethical blindspot* explosive, or a *temptation* explosive. Either way, one wrong move has the potential for extreme danger.

To avoid those unnecessary landmines, there has to be a commitment to exemplary leadership. Leaders need leadership standards. They must put aside their own needs and desires to engage in the actual responsibilities of being a leader. Both the leader and the team must be willing to hold each other accountable through accountability partnerships.

Accountability Partner(s)

People have accountability partners for everything ranging from weight loss to new projects or ventures. Accountability partners help make sure that partners stay on task and focus on their goals. Accountability partners help individuals successfully uphold their commitment and most importantly, they redirect these individuals when they start to waiver. Accountability partners can be mentors as well, but they are not the same. Mentors typically specialize in your area of leadership, whereas an accountability partner can be anyone trusted enough to be your voice of reason.

It is beneficial to have an accountability partner for your leadership brand. It is not only necessary to ensure that someone is there to keep you out of trouble, but an accountability partner offers unbiased and sound guidance along the leadership journey. There is nothing shameful or limiting about seeking guidance. Pride is a massive hindrance to achieving any goal; and prideful leaders are limited and less effective in their progress.

Accountability involves humility. Leaders need people who will keep them humble! Humility is an understanding that even as the leader, you don't have all the answers. You are not invincible, and you need others to help you lead well. Even if it is just one person, someone needs to be empowered to freely say, "I don't think that's a good idea." The problem is that because of the authority associated with leadership, leaders sometimes intimidate those who genuinely try to advise them. They surround themselves with their *yes crowd*, which results in the leader doing whatever he/she wants to do.

An accountability partner assesses the leader's situation with a clear and unbiased perspective. They can possess clearer mindsets about certain circumstances and offer sound advice. No one achieves success alone. Everyone needs someone who will help them by listening, advising, observing, and providing an objective opinion. Seeking guidance is not an indicator of poor leadership ability or insufficiency. It is an acknowledgment of a desire for growth and improvement. Leadership without guidance can be disastrous.

Leaders are also held accountable through governing bodies and systems. These structures provide checks and balances to ensure that leaders operate effectively and ethically. Further, governing bodies help to ensure leaders do not easily fall into the temptations that will undoubtedly present. Boards or advisory groups are examples of this type of entity.

If leaders would fully adopt a legitimate system that is designed to hold themselves to their promises and actions, the perception of leaders may change and redirect toward a more positive and beneficial path.

Establish ethics standards. There are key aspects necessary for changing the unethical culture that is rapidly spreading throughout leadership. They serve as a guide throughout the ethical journey and help leaders avoid pitfalls.

Most people value stability and this priority is no different in leadership. Comfort, security, and productivity dwell in stable environments. In addition to other responsibilities, leaders are responsible for establishing a sense of stability and creating an environment where their followers can thrive. This begins with establishing fixed points or guiding principles in decision-making.

We've discussed the possibilities for why ethical leadership has taken a less positive turn but establishing tangible solutions to this issue is key to producing results. One solution is to create customized ethical standards for your leadership environment. Without clear guiding points of reference, leaders begin to make their own rules and can quickly lose control. Leaders should establish a baseline code of ethical standards that are embraced by all stakeholders within an organization and are part of the leadership brand. Setting these standards involves a proactive approach to resolving ethical leadership issues.

The ethical standards should not only be established, but they should also be updated and reviewed regularly as a priority. For leaders with teams, it is critical to communicate these standards regularly. Remember that your behaviors and actions result in a reflection of your leadership brand. As technology and the environment change and innovate, so will your standards. Though your values can be unwavering, as society continues to change, understanding your potential vulnerabilities is important. It gives you a head start of remaining focused on the ethical direction that you desire.

For those with teams, it is also the responsibility of everyone who represents your leadership brand and business to ensure that the ethical standards established are applied. It becomes a team effort. The code of ethics is the ethical standards with which anyone representing the organization must comply.

The ethical standards can include anything from conflicts of interest, checks and balances within the organization, appropriate and inappropriate relationships as well as other variables. These standards should be customized based on your values, environment and culture.[53] Remember that the goal is to set boundaries and establish a shared understanding of values.

Develop moral and ethical leaders. The best way to change a culture is to train and develop the next generation. This is where leadership influence comes into the picture. Well-respected leaders are capable of creating a tremendous impact. People admire the character and integrity of a well-respected leadership model.

President Jimmy Carter served one term as president of the United States and is not often credited as the most effective U.S. president. Despite that, he is highly well-respected for his leadership that has proven farther- reaching than his work as president. He is known for his global humanitarian work, ethical and moral standing, and dedication to his mission. Sometimes the "good" behaviors of the leader create a more substantial impact than even the leader's expertise. President Carter is a fitting example of this because his brand evolved from a former president to a leader who has gained the respect of individuals and world leaders alike.

By practicing your own Code of Ethics, future leaders are exposed to your important values.[54] Not only do they learn these values, but they also continue to emphasize and exemplify those values because of your influence. Remember, the first example comes from the leader and then followed by those who are influenced by the leader's actions. In time, what seemed like your own values will establish a new culture of leadership and become the norm. This exemplifies leadership at its finest: influence derived by the courageous, unprecedented actions of the leader.

Avoiding the bad is not the same as upholding the good. Taking proactive measures to become an ethical leader ensures that your brand upholds ethical behaviors and serves as a baseline measurement and training system for current and future leadership brands. As time continues and leadership models further evolve, it is imperative that your levels of power and influence work intentionally to help change the leadership culture and reestablish the respect and integrity of the role.

By now, I'm sure that you can connect how your leadership responsibility correlates to your leadership behavior and the value of your leadership brand. These principles build trust and respect. Ethical leaders are better able to connect, influence, and develop relationships with others because they are trustworthy. As a leader, it is so important to consider the magnitude of your potential impact. Your influence is powerful and a valuable contribution to the leadership conversation. Be sure to use that impact wisely.

Self-serving leadership brands result in deception and exploitation of others rather than the genuine achievement of impactful results.[55] Poor leadership behaviors result in pitfalls that can transform organizations. Unethical leadership brands often cause divisiveness. Focusing on ethical behavior and the accountability model draws invaluable outcomes that unify, sustain, and positively impact.

Ethical leadership brands have the potential for a powerful reputation of influence. They can produce results that yield high performance, high numbers of followers, high employee morale, highly respected brands, and a long-lasting legacy for others to model. The benefits are indeed endless and further reaching than consequences associated with more adverse leadership behaviors.

Chapter 6

ACTING ETHICALLY

"Your leadership, good or bad, will make a huge difference."[56] – John Cantwell

We've come to a point in our discussion that I believe is pivotal. We've already looked at some key leadership styles and theories; and we've discussed the need for a new perspective and interpretation of leadership. Our journey continued with recognizing leadership as a personal brand. Then we came to understand that the influential abilities of a leader determine the measure of leadership effectiveness. Such influence is based upon his/her actions while the type of influence is categorized by ethical or unethical behaviors.

While research shows that the possession of certain traits alone does not guarantee leadership success, there is evidence that effective leaders are different from other people in certain key respects;[57] particularly honesty and integrity. Remember, influence is not determined by good or bad leadership. As our chapter quote suggests, good or bad leadership still makes an impact.

Ethical leaders possess similar characteristics that others find reputable, admirable, and an effective leadership style. In our discussion of ethical leadership, we've looked at examples of these leaders and the tools and strategies to help ensure that you, the leader, remain committed to your ethical leadership brand. Doing so is beneficial and effective in achieving your leadership goals.

So, what's next? *Applying* ethics *to* your leadership brand is the next step. Possessing certain traits is only a precondition for effective leadership. Action is key! There are four important actions that exemplary leaders can take in order to help safeguard their ethical qualities. These include realizing your responsibility, developing value statements, creating a proactive strategy, and being the change.

Realizing Your Responsibility

Earlier, we discussed the responsibility of leadership. Now is the time for you to apply this understanding to your leadership brand. As an ethical leader, it's necessary to realize that *you* set the standard for appropriate behaviors and actions. Essentially, ethics requires a healthy gauge of what's right across all platforms. This means considering how you treat others, how you handle business, your vision, and how you conduct yourself when others are not observing you.

Ethical leaders must understand and proactively consider the consequences of their actions. It is easy to become consumed in the moment, react impulsively, and make irrational decisions that yield long-term consequences. However, realizing the immense responsibility of leadership and holding firm to the foundational beliefs and values that you established will help in pivotal decision-making.

Develop Values Statements

For an exemplary leader, beliefs, principles, and values are the basis for ethical leadership.[58] Developing values statements help you govern yourself and commit to your ideals. When faced with potentially brand-damaging circumstances or difficult decisions in general, ethical leaders assess the potential effects of their decisions. The values statement communicates, in writing, what you believe in and stand for. It is your commitment to yourself and those with whom your impact affects.

When developing values statements consider the top five to seven values that mean the most to you. Create phrases and short sentences that are specific to your value commitment. Your values statements are declarations that help establish a healthy and realistic sense of who you are.

One value statement of Uber Technologies, Inc., the multinational ride-sharing company proclaims, "We do the right thing. Period."[59] This is a very direct reflection of their desired brand reputation. Similarly, a Johnson and Johnson, Inc. values statement declares, "We must be good citizens."[60] This represents their commitment to corporate social responsibility. One compelling values statement comes from St. Jude Children's Research Hospital which proclaims, "No child is denied treatment."[61] This statement is the foundation for the pediatric research hospital and the core of its existence. As with these examples, your values should also be specific reflections of your commitments.

Creating a Proactive Strategy

The next step is to strategize by assessing potential decisions proactively. Being proactive means thinking about possible scenarios even before they are presented. In order to thoroughly assess your choices, develop questions to ask yourself that will help in future decision-making. The responses to your questions should align with your values statement. When faced with difficult decisions you can easily refer to your questions and values statements for guidance on the next steps. It's best to decide on the choices that align with the standards that you create. These questions can be as specific or generic as necessary. They can include:

- What is the *right* thing to do?

- How are people affected by my actions?[62]

- How is my brand affected by my actions?

- Will these actions harm others or the business?

- Is this something that I would want others to find out about?

- What would be the impact if this story hit the headlines?

- Would my followers and team be proud of my actions?

- Can my brand survive the fallout?

Thoughtful consideration of the outcomes of these starter questions allow leaders an opportunity to pause, reflect, and process the best decisions before responding.

Making the right decisions ultimately results in a more trustworthy leadership brand. Trust is critical to the leadership brand as it catalyzes healthy relationships between the ethical leader, followers, and the public. When followers believe in a leader, they feel obligated to reciprocate their leader's favor and internalize the leader's values and beliefs.[63] The result is influence based on the actions of an exemplary, ethical leader.

Be the Change

As we continue the discussion of exemplary leaders, I'd like to introduce additional actions that ethical leaders can use to build an effective, personal leadership brand. These are the Five

Practices of Exemplary Leadership as described by leadership authors Kouzes and Posner. They consist of actions commonly found in several different types of leadership styles. Exemplifying these actions align with the concept of "practicing what you preach." Leaders following these models are mostly considered exemplary because their actions align with their words. The Five Practices of Exemplary Leadership include:[64]

1. Modeling the way.

2. Inspiring a shared vision.

3. Challenging the process.

4. Enabling others to act.

5. Encouraging the heart.

These practices serve as a beneficial guide to the application of ethical and exemplary leadership. They also contribute to the potential impact of the leadership brand.

Modeling the Way

Modeling the way is mainly action-based and situational.[65] It involves the leader's ability to adjust the leadership style in order to be the most effective. This practice is based on the leader's flexibility and understanding of the needs of their environment. Effective leaders can modify their style based on the requirements necessary to meet their goals by influencing others. They understand that there is no basic approach to leadership and that to be exemplary means leading by example.

A fitting example of modeling the way leadership is husband and wife team, Terence and Cecilia Lester, founders of a non-profit organization called Love Beyond Walls. Located in metropolitan Atlanta, Georgia, the organization advocates across the country on behalf of those who are impoverished. Their leadership style serves as a model due to the hands-on, servant leadership example that they set for their team.

Rather than *talking* about the homeless issue, they are actively involved in grassroots efforts to help eradicate homelessness and poverty while addressing the immediate needs of vulnerable populations. Outreach efforts such as sleeping under bridges with the homeless and solely enduring a two-month walk from Atlanta, Georgia to Washington, DC gained national attention as many following the journey contributed to the growth and success of their cause.

The impact of this exemplary leadership has resulted in 97,319 people resourced with basic needs over the past six years.[66] They have a growing staff that is committed to the organization and, as a result of their efforts, they have provided housing, shelter, and successful national advocacy campaigns on behalf of the impoverished. The model of leading by example has been far-reaching for this organization and, in most cases more, impactful than leading with words. During the unprecedented COVID-19 pandemic, for example, Love Beyond Walls received global recognition as leading advocates for the homeless population. The group placed portable handwashing stations, supplied with soap and water, to the highest traffic homeless areas across the nation. The group also picks up the stations daily, disinfects and refills each with water and soap.[67] Their efforts were have been modeled around the world.

Kouzes and Posner talk specifically about how a leader's deeds are far more important than their words.[68] If we think of our own relationships with our leaders, this is certainly the case. Modeling the way is an illustration of the commitment to the vision and to the people. No longer does *do as I say and not as I do* work for authority figures. Followers now prefer leaders to *lead through action*.

Inspiring a Shared Vision

Inspiring a shared vision first requires envisioning the future by imagining exciting and ennobling possibilities.[69] This practice is concerned primarily with influence. The leader has the vision and the followers breathe life into it because they are inspired and influenced to believe in it.

Dr. Martin Luther King Jr.'s leadership during the civil rights movement is a fitting example of inspiring a vision. As indicated in his "I Have a Dream" speech, he led a movement by influencing others that the day of equality and social justice was on the horizon even though the circumstances at that time suggested otherwise. Remember, leadership is not solely about a position or authority. It is mainly about influence and impact. The civil rights movement grew because others were influenced to believe in the vision and act in an impactful way.

Leadership does not happen alone. The more a leader exemplifies ethical practices and an understanding of the leadership responsibility, the more followers will develop and assist in efforts to achieve the vision. Inspiring a vision first requires establishing and communicating the vision—a topic that we will explore in detail in a later chapter.

Challenging the Process

The main theme that resonates from the practice of challenging the process is igniting a change from the status quo. This means that you take a chance on an uncharted path. Leaders must be courageous and innovative. Challenging the process is a beneficial practice for ethical leaders as it means that leaders are not accepting of the customary.[70]

Ethical leaders challenge the unethical practices that tend to overshadow exemplary leadership models. They move away from mediocre, self-serving, and status quo leadership to create a new leadership model based on honesty, ethics, sacrifice, and service. Doing things differently, thoughtfully, ethically, respectfully, and strategically, are ways to apply this process to your leadership brand. We need to see more leaders with the courage to challenge the process and stand for what is right no matter how unpopular it may seem or how isolated the leader feels.

Challenging the process is largely an authentic leadership practice. It requires *acting* differently and blazing uncharted territory. Authentic leadership requires four main attributes of confidence, hope, optimism, and resilience. Challenging the process strengthens those qualities and is a key catalyst to change.

Enabling Others to Act / Encouraging the Heart

Enabling others to act and encouraging the heart are both primarily associated with transformational leadership.[71] I believe that they are the sum result of modeling the way, inspiring a vision, and challenging the process. They are comprised of inspirational motivation, idealized influence, individualized consideration, and intellectual stimulation.[72] Motivated by the acceptance of change in customs and structure, the ability to enable others to act and also encourage others means that not only do followers trust the leader, but they also believe in the vision.

Enabling others to act is a sign of influence and a transfer of leadership power. If leadership begins with action and if through leadership qualities, you enable others also to act, then, in essence, you the leader are effective. Enabling others to act means that the leader's influence was so dominating and impactful that it sparked action in others. Encouraging the heart translates to compassion. It is understanding what others need to be successfully led, then working to ensure that they receive what is needed. Both practices require sacrifice, self-awareness and the ability to influence.

The leadership model for becoming an ethical leader through exemplary action requires a combination of the complex leadership qualities that represent your leadership brand. In order to apply this model of leadership, leaders must engage with others and create a connection that increases motivation and drive to move beyond the customary. Stakeholders and followers alike must trust the leader to move them from a secure and familiar understanding of customary beliefs, products, or a cause to a place of unfamiliarity and vulnerability.[73] The challenge is that while stakeholders expect the leader to lead, they don't always trust the methods or abilities of the leader to do so effectively.

We discussed previously that the Office of the President is respected regardless of whether or not we respect the person holding that office. One idea that leaders must remember is that, initially, you have your followers' attention just out of respect for the leadership role. What you do with that attention, from your behaviors, actions, encounters, and decision-making, is crucial to your success and influence as a leader. It is also important to have committed followers in order to implement your leadership plans successfully.

As we move into the upcoming chapters, we will discuss just how crucial followers are to your impact as a leader. But our very next step is to make sure you are aware of the characteristics that comprise your own identity in order to customize your leadership brand.

Chapter 7

DEFINING YOUR LEADERSHIP BRAND

"To be authentic is literally to be your own author, to discover your own native energies and desires, and then to find your own way of acting on them."[74] - Warren Bennis

The above quote perfectly summarizes the objective of this chapter, which is to help you define your authentic, distinguishable leadership brand. Now that we have established an understanding of leadership from a personal branding perspective and observed the potential of ethical leadership, it is time to focus on you, the leader. It's time to unfold the potential of your brand by recognizing and customizing your own leadership qualities. These qualities will comprise your personal leadership brand.

To begin, let's examine a critical and foundational question: Who are you? Has anyone ever asked you that? Perhaps you may have even asked yourself that question. Either way, answering this seemingly simple question is not always easy. In fact, understanding who you are and discovering your strengths and weaknesses can be complex.

Recognizing the Impact of Your Leadership Brand

Considering that there are approximately 200 different types of cells in the human body and over 37 trillion total cells that in some capacity contribute to who we are as individuals,[75] complex is no understatement. Similarly, your leadership DNA is just as complicated with a combination of the many aspects of you from exposures to experiences, behaviors, and interactions. Together, these factors and others contribute to attributes that shape your leadership brand.

As we've discussed, your leadership brand is an authentic reflection of who you are as a person and as a leader. It is what differentiates you from others. Your leadership brand communicates your value and is the catalyst for building trust. Given how interconnected leadership is to the person, it is surprising that leadership brand development is often overlooked in leadership conversations. A poorly developed leadership brand can be detrimental to the leader's goals and impact. A powerful leadership brand however, can help broaden and deepen the leader's results and influence.

Leaders are generally considered effective based on evaluations of their operational and functional capabilities. However, given the increasingly competitive climate and more opportunities for exposure through changing technologies, globalization, and innovations, it is imperative that leaders interested in longevity, growth, and divergence develop an ongoing strategic thought process about their leadership style. They should formulate intentional tactics to lead effectively.

The Brand New Leader

Establishing the leadership brand is a foundational asset to achieving leadership goals while building the leader's confidence. Remember this, whether or not you explore and align your personal attributes with your leadership style, who you are as a person will still emerge. It is best to examine your qualities, maximize your strengths, and build on your weakness to improve your leadership potential.

The goal of this chapter is to provide tools to help you customize your authentic brand as a leader. So how do you determine the answer to the infamous question: Who are you? A parallel to this question is: What kind of leader are you? The search for the answer is not easy. Assessing strengths and weaknesses; and then working to overcome them is difficult. However, doing so creates endless possibilities.

Warren Bennis states, "If knowing yourself and being yourself were as easy to do as to talk about, there wouldn't be nearly so many people walking around in borrowed postures, spouting secondhand ideas, trying desperately to fit in rather than to stand out."[76] Your leadership brand should not fit in; it should stand out. Remember that leaders are courageous in pursuing unprecedented actions which begins with the leadership style. Your leadership brand can be distinguishable based on self-awareness and alignment with the qualities that you possess.

Recognizing the Impact of Your Leadership Brand

Self-awareness involves a conscious understanding of one's personality and individuality.[77] The word conscious also means intentional. Everything about leadership is intentional, especially the development of the brand. Once leadership is established — meaning that actions have generated influence — the next steps should be strategic and purposeful in the quest for self-discovery.

Because leadership comes in so many forms, approaches, and styles, one can easily lose focus on their own leadership brand. In the sea of what can seem like the more popular and effective leadership styles and standards, having confidence in your brand eliminates the opportunity to become consumed with others. Leaders must have a firm grasp of their brand, or else they can become vulnerable to what I refer to as a leadership identity crisis.

The leadership identity crisis usually occurs because someone else's style of leadership produces what seems to be more desirable outcomes. As a result, other leaders mimic in hopes of achieving similar outcomes. The problem is that if your leadership brand is not authentic to you or the environment in which you lead, the results will not be as impactful. One size does not fit all in leadership. With a good sense of self-awareness, leaders are able to avoid the identity crisis and build a leadership brand that benefits their needs.

Self-awareness is vital in leadership. It allows you to pay attention to how your actions, reactions, and interactions affect your influence. Notice the prevalence of the root word *action*. As we have discussed, action is the foundation of leadership. There is no leadership without action. A leader should constantly *do* in order to influence; and action is pivotal throughout the leadership process.

The Leadership B.R.A.N.D. Assessment

Action is an important linkage between self-awareness and leadership. Self-awareness involves *you* understanding yourself. The next step consists of using that understanding to maximize the positive outcomes of your leadership brand. It is also connected to determining a distinctive identity. To help increase self-awareness of attributes that positively impact the leadership brand, I've developed the Leadership BRAND Assessment.

The Leadership BRAND Assessment is a leadership identity assessment tool. This tool helps identify specific leadership determinants that aid in the intentional and strategic development of your personal leadership brand. It offers an opportunity to explore avenues that will enhance your understanding of yourself and improve your leadership potential.

LEADERSHIP B.R.A.N.D ASSESSMENT

IDENTIFYING QUALITIES THAT DEFINE YOUR LEADERSHIP BRAND.

B **BELIEFS**
- What principles do I stand for?
- What do I value most?
- What qualities do I expect from others?
- What are my uncompromising beliefs?

R **REACTIONS**
- How do others view my brand?
- How can I best manage my response?
- My leadership style ignites what reactions?
- What are my methods of influence?

A **ABILITIES**
- What are areas in which I excel?
- What do I love about my work?
- What do people ask of me the most?
- In which of my abilities am I most confident?

N **NEGATIVES**
- What potential pitfalls should I consider?
- What leadership skills do I lack?
- Which skills need developing?
- What are my most pressing challenges?

D **DISTINCTIONS**
- What are my most distinct qualities?
- Which qualities are most recognized?
- What strengths enhance my leadership style?
- What resources are available to enhance my brand?

The Write Media Group, LLC.

In the assessment, each letter of BRAND represents a determinant of leadership brand effectiveness. BRAND is an acronym for **B**eliefs, **R**eactions, **A**bilities, **N**egatives, and **D**istinctions. Your brand effectiveness is determined by your beliefs, reactions to your actions, your abilities, and how you use them. The negatives are also huge determinants of your brand's effectiveness. The negatives that you encounter and possess, and the way in which you respond to them all contribute to your effectiveness. Lastly, and equally as important are your distinctions. The factors that make your brand distinct become how you are recognized and what you are recognized for. All determinants are valuable to developing your leadership brand and together, they help create an awareness that leads to the authentic brand that represents you.

Answering targeted questions related to each determinant helps increase leaders' self-awareness. It also helps to proactively consider unrealized possibilities. This tool helps leaders better customize their brands while becoming more mindful of who they are and how they will lead. This assessment helps produce confidence in the brand. That confidence helps leaders remain unwavering when faced with temptations and pressures. We will explore each element specifically.

Beliefs

The Beliefs determinant addresses the idea of leadership values and the ethics variables that we discussed in earlier chapters. Establishing your leadership beliefs calls for sincere moments of self awareness. You should strongly consider your answer to the questions listed in the Beliefs section. You may also think of other similar questions to help you further discover your beliefs.

Consider aspects such as your leadership Code of Ethics, your vision, the areas in which you wish to remain accountable and other areas that address *your* ideologies. The key is to remember that each response is specific to you. Think about how your responses relate to your role as a leader and the pros and cons of each. Everything that you believe in or value may not mesh well into your overall brand. On the contrary, you may be challenged to establish or develop certain values that are necessary for your specific leadership goals. For those who may struggle to establish values, think about what makes you uncomfortable and what you would like to change as a leader. Values are created by understanding what you will not stand for. Prioritize your beliefs and consider the best way to incorporate them into your brand.

For example, Chick-fil-A founder Truett Cathy decided to close all stores on Sundays based on what he describes as his Christian beliefs and values. Cathy noted that closing on

Sunday demonstrates his loyalty to the Lord.[78] Despite pressures to remain competitive and follow other business models, the Chick-fil-A brand remains committed to its stance.

Cathy's beliefs helped distinguish his leadership brand and ultimately resulted in business success and impact. Similarly, your beliefs and values should also be unwavering. They should encompass the factors that are important and represent you. Values and beliefs serve as a guide for decision-making and a model to remain ethical and set guidelines for your brand.

Your beliefs should help you clarify and make explicit the ethical and decision-making parameters of decisions and judgment.[79] After all, one of the many responsibilities of leadership is to uphold the set of ethics and norms that govern the behaviors and cultures of organizations. Beliefs are an important aspect of your leadership character. The definition of character is the mental and moral qualities distinctive to an individual.[80] The best example of character is how a person *acts* when no one is watching. It is an indicator of how you will lead once your actions generate a response.

Beliefs are vital to effective leadership. Thoughtfully analyzing your beliefs and merging those into your leadership brand contributes to the practical development of your leadership brand.

Reactions

The Reaction determinant reflects another measure of leadership effectiveness based on the current or potential response to leadership actions. In this determinant, you will analyze how the people, industry, or environments, perceive and respond to your leadership brand. It is helpful for leaders to understand the effectiveness of their leadership styles, approaches, and interactions as it aids in their development, improvement, and effectiveness across various groups. You will assess the cultural factors in which you lead; and based on those evaluations, determine what type of response your brand solicits.

The Reactions determinant is important for many reasons. First, leadership begins — and ends – with action. It starts with your action and ends with the actions of others that are motivated by your impact. A true measure of your leadership effectiveness is how others respond to your actions. Are others motivated to improve and work harder, or do they feel frustrated and discouraged? The reaction demonstrates your level of influence. When evaluating responses to the questions in this section, consider whether or not your responses align with what you desire and, if not, think of strategies to ensure an alignment. In addition to the assessment questions, you may also consider the questions below.

- What do people think of me?

- What responses do I desire and how can I adjust my brand to solicit those?

- What are the undesirable responses that I observe and what role does my brand play in those?

- What do I typically inspire and what are my methods of influence?

The Reactions determinant is another example of the need for mindful and conscious leaders. As a leader, you must be aware of the effects of your brand. Does your brand create anxiety, confusion, or low morale? Or, does it ignite a positive response to your call-to-action? You must be aware of how you make people feel –positively or negatively—and how you communicate your messages, strategies, and vision. Mindful leaders know their strengths and weaknesses and how those attributes work or do not work in the leadership context.

Many of the answers to your Reactions questions are based on follower and/or environmental responses. Think of this section as a process for collecting, quantifying, and reporting the observations of others concerning you. We will discuss followership in an upcoming chapter, as followers are also vital to the leadership brand. However, leaders without a team can also complete this assessment to become more proactive and thoughtful about the potential and desired reactions to leadership style. Another piece of this assessment is to help you develop your own questions that are specific to your personal leadership scenario.

Abilities

Understanding your abilities helps you discover necessary areas of growth and development. This understanding is beneficial to develop an accurate, well-rounded interpretation of yourself as an individual and as a leader. Evaluating your abilities is a way to identify your strengths and the specific attributes that contribute to leadership effectiveness. The abilities that you define can build into strengths once the correct efforts for enhancement occur. The first step involves realizing your potential through an awareness of your abilities.

Abilities can derive from anything from your most effective leadership style, your talents, specialties, experiences, and backgrounds. The Abilities determinant is an assessment of the skills derived from such factors. For instance, the ability to communicate well can potentially develop into a leadership strength of effective communication. The ability to handle multiple tasks well can develop into the leadership strength of effectively multitasking. Awareness of your abilities, as well as your areas needed for improvement, positively increases your knowledge and enhances the most effective behaviors in leadership. Noting, monitoring, and consistently taking the necessary steps to build your abilities provides an opportunity for consistency in measurement and reporting of growth and outcomes.

Research suggests that key leadership strengths include areas such as self- awareness and mindfulness, communication, collaboration, relatability, decision-making, strategy, and vision, to name a few. As we've already established, courage, innovation, and confidence are also dominant strengths of leadership. The next step is to answer a few starter questions from the BRAND assessment in order to identify areas that align with key strengths as well as your own abilities that will enhance your leadership brand.

Remember, leadership effectiveness is established once an *action* ignites influence. Thinking through your abilities, improving on your weaknesses and aligning those traits with your leadership brand are actions that help distinguish you as a leader. While a leader is influential in the forward progression of a process through action, the forward progress happens through the leader's *abilities*.

Negatives

The Negatives determinant is probably the most beneficial category of the assessment because it helps leaders become aware of potential obstacles –something imperative in leadership. I like to think of this determinant as proactive crisis preparedness. It is the category that helps you consider and prepare for the obstacles and barriers that are inevitable throughout your leadership journey. No crystal ball can predict what is to come. However, thoughtful preparation before a roadblock occurs is a valuable strategy to implement.

Negatives include any opposing forces with the potential to block your successful leadership outcomes. They occur at any moment and at any point within the journey. All leaders should prepare for the unexpected. Preparation begins with thoughtful strategies to avoid and overcome pitfalls. Developing a plan to do so helps build leadership confidence when implementation becomes necessary. Just as with disaster and emergency preparedness strategies, prepare a response to all potential barriers.

During a crisis, leaders look to their crisis plan, which is a set of strategies to implement when such situations occur. Having a plan eliminates the need to figure out what to do at the time of the crisis. The plan enables leaders to *act* — or lead, rather than react and panic. This preparedness happens because the leaders have already considered the possible situation and had the appropriate lead time to develop a meaningful strategy.

During the COVID-19 pandemic, for example, many school systems scrambled to create a plan that would allow their students to receive the same quality education at home as they would in an in-person setting. Although this was a challenge for everyone, some schools handled the transition better than others. Notably, one school transitioned well primarily because they had a plan already in place for similar situations. Previously, the school developed a remote learning model designed for inclement weather days. After receiving news of the need to shelter-in-place indefinitely, leadership decided to expand the inclement weather plan and use it as a pandemic model.

As a result, the school's remote learning transition and implementation happened reasonably seamlessly. This caused the parents, students, and staff to feel more confident in the school's leadership and future decisions and actions concerning the pandemic. Recognizing that leaders will not always have an opportunity to prepare for the unexpected, proactively identifying potential barriers is the best practice. The preparedness strategy helps leaders respond quickly and efficiently while also building trust in their leadership abilities.

The Negatives determinant takes into consideration any possible barriers, including financial, situational, physical, or any other roadblock specific to the environment. Think of this as your leadership brand preparedness playbook. Regarding the leadership brand, such questions to consider may include the following.

The Negatives determinant does not just include stereotypically negative areas; this category can also include anything that could be a potential barrier from skills that need improvement, staffing challenges, financial challenges, or specific situations. This area is another category that will be customized for your particular circumstances. Many of the questions in the Negatives determinant may be opposite of those in the Abilities determinant. For instance, if a question about abilities includes, *"In what areas do I excel?"* The Negatives determinant may include the question, *"In what areas am I most challenged?"* Contrasting the two determinants helps create a more valid assessment.

Distinctions

The Distinctions determinant is a category filled with concepts that we have covered and will continue to cover throughout this book. Despite this recurring theme however, this category may be the most difficult to complete. It is challenging for most people to assess themselves accurately. Either we will be overly critical in our assessment, or we will underestimate our need to improve in certain areas. Self-assessment, however, can occur accurately with tailored questions, honesty, and an unbiased look at self. These are strategies that will especially help you determine your distinctions — the most defining aspect of your leadership brand.

Knowing your *why* is almost as challenging as selling your *why* to others.[81] Assessing your distinctions involves unpacking and then repacking *you* so that your *why* best reflects your personality, professionalism, and value as a leader.[82] Identifying your distinctions involves looking at yourself differently. Your personal leadership brand should be a realistic interpretation of you. Leadership influence cannot occur until there is some level of personal connection and/or relatability between the influencer and those being influenced. As the influencer, your brand should stand out as distinctive. It should offer something new and uncustomary.

Identifying your distinctions require a conversation with yourself and others. It also requires the courage to be authentic. Some of the characteristics that you identify may not seem fitting for a leader. However, those are the distinctions that will set your brand apart. The Distinctions determinant challenges you to be a visionary. It helps fine-tune the aspects of your brand that will be the most personal and genuine, as well as influential to others. Your distinctions represent honesty as well as vulnerability regarding who you are. Follow each response to your Distinctions determinants with methods for how you will merge them into a customized personal brand.

The insights developed from your Leadership BRAND assessment are thought-provoking tools to not only help you customize your leadership brand but also help you recognize your value. Leadership generates impact and the individual tools that you possess are catalysts for the potential impact of your brand on your industry and possibly the world.

Mark Zuckerberg, the co-founder of Facebook, is listed fourth in the Forbes Billionaires list[83]. Zuckerberg started Facebook at the age of 19 at Harvard University. Though only a student at the time, his actions changed the way we all interact on a global scale. Our reaction to his action? Facebook is now one of the largest social networks in the world. In fact, if Facebook were a country, it would be larger than China. India's Facebook audience alone would be ranked fourth in terms of the largest populations worldwide![84] That's an impact that is way stronger than an undergraduate student who was enjoying a hobby.

Zuckerberg's initial leadership actions were based on his personal strengths, abilities, and interests. His leadership brand transitioned him into an influential global leader and ignited a global response to his leadership.

The response to your brand can generate an impact that becomes larger than even the leader. Identifying elements that enhance your brand's distinction will help you become more confident, self-aware, and distinguishable. It is important to note that there are no right or wrong answers to this assessment. The goal is to help you take a deep dive into possible qualities and attributes that you may not have otherwise considered.

These prompts should help you discover, build, and maximize qualities that will distinguish your leadership brand.

The answers to this assessment become parts of the strategy that you will develop that will boost your leadership impact. With your potential impact largely based on your influence, it is now time to discuss your most valuable asset to your leadership brand: your followers.

Chapter 8

FOLLOWERS: YOUR GREATEST ASSET

"Exemplary leadership is impossible without full inclusion of the follower."[85] – Warren Bennis

Leadership is the core of every success talk. It is a lesson that has been emphasized throughout our entire lives. As children, we were taught to *be a leader and not a follower*. The goal was to instill confidence in our individuality and potential. Our parents and teachers wanted to ensure that we did not conform to peer pressure or adopt a mindset of fitting in with a crowd.

Though motivated by the best intentions, subliminally, these and other pro-leadership declarations enforced an underlying stigma regarding followership. The impression left by such messages was that followers are less than leaders. It is worth noting that in leadership research and within the context of this book, followership does not carry that same stigma or negative connotation. Here, followership is a term that is celebrated and valued.

The *follower* is considered an equal, if not a more valuable, contributor to leadership effectiveness. Yes, leaders are essential, but followers are also. Followers create results, carry out the leader's vision, and can transition into outstanding leaders.

While the leadership messages are important, leaders must understand that the best asset and catalyst for success lies within their team of followers. No leader succeeds alone. Even in stories of leaders who built empires from scratch, they still had a team of people helping somewhere along the journey. It is highly difficult to succeed as a leadership brand with no help. While the action of leadership may be solitary, the influence requires others. Realizing the benefits of follower inclusion by maximizing a healthy, professional relationship with followers is a crucial leadership concept that needs attention.

Throughout this book, we have discussed the formula for achieving influence by developing an impactful leadership brand. First, leadership is personal and begins with an action. Then, the action leads to influence, which results in impact. There is one crucial component missing from this formula however; and that's the role of the follower. Somewhere between influence and impact are followers who can help catapult your vision and strategies to dimensions that you may not have considered.

Recognizing the Impact of Your Leadership Brand

The leader/follower relationship is a powerful dynamic within the leadership conversation. Until recently, follower value was often overlooked. Now however, more research exists that emphasizes the contributions of the follower role.

The introductory chapter quote from leadership expert Warren Bennis highlights the fact that full inclusion of the follower is necessary for exemplary leadership. Before we move further, there are two terms requiring explanation: *followership* and *inclusion*. *Followership* refers to an interactive role that others play that complements the leadership role.[86] It includes the *believers* in, and of, the leader and is as important as the leadership role in achieving performance outcomes.

Since influence is a determinant of effective leadership, it makes sense that the inclusion followers is a necessary component of exemplary leadership. A significant factor in the leadership formula is the relationship between leaders and followers. One reason is that leaders need followers in order to influence effectively.

Think about the idea of influence in the context of social media. Followers follow an individual that they consider influential in a specific area. These influencers — as they are often labeled — are now sought after by companies and marketers who realize their vast reach and power of persuasion.[87] This is why social media influencers can earn hundreds of thousands of dollars or more per post. Their number of followers measures their level of influence. They are influencing their followers to buy a product, believe a theory, or utilize a service. These influencers are considered the leaders of social media.

It is understood that leaders hold a position of influence. A leader's abilities, strategies, and actions to achieve that influence -- and the associated outcomes -- are factors that comprise their leadership brand. However, followership is also a vital component of the leadership brand for several reasons that we will discuss.

Let's think again about social media. If social media influencers had no followers, would they be as influential? Would they have any power or voice of persuasion? The answer is *no*. Their influence potential, as well as their earning potential, are based largely on their number of followers. Influencers are not influential without followers to influence. In the same regard, leaders are not influential until they capture the attention of potential followers. With no follower influence, is the leader effective?

Inclusion refers to incorporating the unique and best capabilities of the follower into specific and vital aspects of the leadership strategy. Let's focus in on the unique and best capabilities. Followers are welcomed to the team usually because of their unique qualities and talents. Inclusion refers to the need for leaders to cultivate environments that enhance follower effectiveness. Leaders have a responsibility to create an environment that permits followers to operate freely in their abilities. To do this, leaders must welcome and maximize the capabilities of their followers. They must eliminate the barriers that stifle or exclude followers' true selves. These barriers come in the form of anything that limits followers from thriving.

Many of the key aspects of your brand such as open communication, trust, integrity, development, respect, value, and so many others, open the door to full inclusion. Follower inclusion adds to your brand, so it is important to allow followers the freedom to do their tasks to remain effective. Furthermore, inclusive means creating a welcoming environment rather than forcing followers to conform to a more stifling culture.

Effective leadership branding is not achievable without experiencing measurable results. Measuring leadership effectiveness has proven to be difficult throughout the years, largely because of the various definitions and interpretations of the role. Leadership will most likely never include a single, agreed-upon definition and because of this, considering its impact on followers is a more streamlined leadership measurement tool.

Right now, you may be thinking, "I thought this was a leadership branding book. Why so much praise and attention to the follower?" Here's your answer: because the leader/follower relationship is vital in yielding positive and productive leadership results. Positive leader and follower interactions improve performance, influence, and overall impact.

The Leader/Follower Relationship

Many leadership actions directly impact the follower and vice versa. However, the most important action of a leader is the *acknowledgement of the follower's value.*[88] Research shows that a large number of followers do not feel valued or respected by their leader. Value stems from respect and an outward expression of recognition and appreciation for the follower's contribution.

A study conducted by the *Harvard Business Review* in 2014 notes that *respect* is the single, most important leadership action that affects followers.[89] Feeling respected by leaders was more vital to followers than even rewards and recognition![90] Respect was also more important to the follower than the leader's vision, and even their own professional development.[91]

Since it is such a critical and defining action, let us pause for a moment and discuss respect. Leaders and followers alike should abide by the rule that we learned as children: *treat others the way that you would like to be treated.* Regardless of rank, status, or position, everyone deserves sincere regard and consideration. Followers are skilled professionals who are people first and should be treated as such. They deserve and desire genuine courtesy and acknowledgement of their effort.

If leadership is viewed from a partnership perspective, rather than, in some cases, a command and control-style relationship, mutual respect is achieved, and so are greater performance results. Judgment, harsh criticism, intimidation, yelling, and blatant disregard for the work and efforts of the team, will crush employee morale and the organizational culture. On the other hand, demonstrating value, acknowledging contributions, encouragement, and coaching generate more significant results than the *iron fist*. This means that leaders with limited resources can still retain loyal and high-achieving followers and, they can achieve outstanding performance outcomes by demonstrating respect to their followers.

No leader is promised a large team. Regardless of staffing limitations, however, loyal and committed followers are not exclusive to large corporate leaders. They are attainable for any leader. Loyalty is achieved when the team recognizes that their leader values their efforts and considers them as a vital asset. Many leaders have achieved success with a small team of followers because followers, for various reasons, buy-*in* to the leadership brand.

This is a fitting opportunity to discuss the law of buy-in. According to the law, which is the 14th of the 21 Irrefutable

Laws of Leadership, "people buy-in to the leader first, then the vision."[92] Your followers have to believe *you,* the leader, before they begin to believe in your vision or strategy. There is no inclusion if there is no buy-in and it all starts with the perception of your leadership brand. Remember, leadership is an action.

Your behavior says a lot about your leadership brand. Followers look for specific qualities from their leaders such as value, respect, communication, vision, and development.[93] We will deal with the rest of these in the next chapters, but it is important to understand that first and foremost, your leadership brand begins with showing respect and value to the follower. Valuing the follower and *communicating* that value is an *action* of leadership.

An exemplary, influential, impactful, successful, and highly-respected leadership brand is so because of the respect and value that is demonstrated to followers. Let me now give you another example of other effects of the leader/follower relationship.

As an employee at a former company, I felt as though I was a valuable contributor to our team. One day, I was walking into the building holding quite a few items. My ability to move quickly was limited due to the heavy load that I was carrying. I struggled a bit but still managed, pretty successfully, to arrive at the front entrance without dropping everything.

Recognizing the Impact of Your Leadership Brand

As I approached the door, a senior leader was headed my way. While within just a few feet of each other, he opened the door first and walked in, never speaking and never looking behind him. At the same time, the door hit me, causing me to drop the items that I successfully carried.

Due to the noise of the collapse, the leader turned slightly, saw me picking up items, turned back around, and headed down the hall. As I gathered my things, I could hear him down the hallway speaking to a fellow *senior* leader. They were chatting about the weekend and engaging in what seemed to be small talk.

What type of impression do you think he, as the leader, left with me? You may read this and think that this was more of a personality issue than a leadership style. But remember, leadership is personal. There is no separation between the person and the leader.

Let's think about what the leader's actions, whether intentional or not, communicated. His actions did not demonstrate value. In fact, it was quite the opposite. From a follower's perspective, that leader's actions impacted my views of my value within the company. While I was confident in my work and abilities, I was not confident that my contributions to the company were valued by leadership. Leaders must be aware and cautious of their contribution to the follower's morale and commitment.

Needless to say, that experience among others, did not help me believe in or *buy-in* to my leader. In fact, my impression of his leadership brand was one of several driving forces behind my decision to leave the company. Followers have to believe you in order to believe *in* you.

So, what traits make a leader believable? There are many, but to name a few, here are some to consider:

- Authenticity: Demonstrating who you are.

- Confidence: Confidence doesn't equal arrogance. It is a demonstration that you are secure and stable in your philosophies, vision, and abilities as a leader.

- Communication: Carefully communicating to your followers and the public with intention.

- Strategy: Having realistic and creative methods to achieve the goals that you define.

In addition to these traits, leaders must make a conscious effort to show value and respect universally to all followers. This includes treating everyone fairly and avoiding the trap of establishing different standards for different individuals. In my experience, it was widely noted and observed that our leader treated his *senior leaders* with more respect than his *worker bees*, as we began to deem ourselves. This type of preferential treatment, known as differentiated leadership, is destructive to the team as well as the leadership brand.

Differentiated Leadership

Differentiated leadership occurs when leaders treat individuals within a group differently.[94] This type of treatment may be unintentional on the part of the leader, but it is highly noticeable by the other members of the team. According to studies, differentiated leadership diminishes group effectiveness, team member self-efficacy, and it lowers group cohesiveness. Your team of followers becomes more divisive and less confident individually.[95] Differentiated leadership also creates a barrier between leaders and followers.

Treating individuals within a group differently deflates the morale and value of followers. This ultimately affects the perception of the leader and the leadership brand. The potential harm of differentiated leadership is not exclusive to large teams. The principles apply to the sole entrepreneur or emerging leader as well because it is based on interactions and relationships with others.

In my example, the people who were feeling ignored and overlooked were the ones doing the boots-on-the-ground work yet receiving no acknowledgement. They were treated noticeably different from others. Although they were the ones staying after-hours and going above and beyond their job descriptions, they also felt obligated to do so just to receive their compensation. Their loyalty was not to their leader's vision or even their organization.

Remember this: there are so many layers of trust that must be developed before followers will buy-in to the vision. If leaders do not establish trust and buy-in early on, loyal employees will lose momentum and eventually leave the leader. Ultimately, the effects include a change in the organizational culture, including high turnover or low employee performance and morale. When such factors occur, leaders should always take a moment to self-reflect and assess what contribution their leadership style played in the situation. Sometimes there is a leadership issue and sometimes not, but in all cases, the leader must take the time to notice the environment and address it.

I have also experienced many exceptional leaders who intentionally showed that they valued and appreciated everyone on their teams. Those teams always thrived. Everyone on the team, no matter the position, wanted to do well not just for the overall organization but also to make sure that our leader shined. We wanted to do our part to ensure that our leader had a positive, external leadership brand. Whereas turnover is high in cultures infused with low employee morale, the more positive leadership experiences yield longevity, sustainability, high performance, and increased morale.[96]

A *Harvard Business Review* study noted that employees who felt respected by their leaders experienced 89 percent greater enjoyment and satisfaction with their jobs and 92 percent greater focus.[97] Also, those employees who felt respected by their leaders were 1.1 times more likely to stay with their company.[98] That means that even with limited resources or limited pay, or challenges and setbacks, respected followers are more likely to remain loyal and help you build your leadership brand.

I recently attended a re-opening event for a business that was previously closed due to structural damage. At the event, the leader continuously praised his team for their commitment to rebuilding the business. He explained that he offered his team extended leave, with pay, as the rebuild occurred. Surprisingly, every team member denied the leave option and chose to help their leader rebuild. As the leader shared this story with such gratitude, it was evident that to garner that level of voluntary commitment from his team; he must have demonstrated that he valued and respected them all.

When followers feel valued, they are more likely to be *engaged* and *committed to* the organizational culture, which is extremely important in the leader and follower relationship and the leadership brand outcomes. The leader and follower dynamic will not exist without mutual respect and appreciation primarily initiated by the leader.

Understand this, leaders and their followers do not have to develop personal friendships or even fraternize excessively. However, even a cordial disposition, a genuine *thank you,* opportunities to hear their feedback, professional development options, or other expressions of value can improve a follower's perspective and improve the leader's brand. Studies show that employees who feel valued and appreciated by their leaders are also more likely to *exceed* expectations.[99] That translates again to loyalty and commitment. What leader doesn't long for loyal and committed followers?

Effective leaders are able to gain respect and establish their position of authority without isolating from their followers or stakeholders. As leadership development initiatives continue to emerge to the forefront of leadership branding strategies, followership concepts should also. If not, the gap between the two becomes wider. Leaders must understand the valuable asset that they have in their followers and work intentionally to cultivate that asset. The leadership brand cannot exist without understanding and intentional strategies to positively influence followers.

Shift in Leadership Power

Another reason to emphasize the value of the follower is that leaders need followers now more than ever before. The 21st century brought about numerous innovations in technological capabilities as well as cultural and philosophical advances.[100] Some believe that these advances are what led to the shift in leadership power which is the transfer of power from the leader to the follower.

Although ultimately, as the leader, you hold an expected level of authority, followers are able to hold leaders more accountable for their actions, tactics, and knowledge than has previously been possible. Just as in our conversation about social media influencers, the power of leadership impact lies within the follower. As we noted, without followers the leader has no influence. Leaders are held to a higher standard now whereas previously in history, leadership culture positioned followers into a more passive role. Because of various factors such as access to technology that forces leadership transparency, personal and professional development, and increased education that allows followers to gain additional knowledge, the power to hold leaders accountable for their actions and outcomes lies within the followers.

The shift in power has also resulted in a leadership culture that is inclusive of situations that may now position followers to serve in a leadership capacity when their own skills, behaviors, or traits deem appropriate. Leaders select, equip, train, and influence one or more followers,[101] hopefully, in a positive and responsible way. As a result, they should have confidence in their followers' abilities to also step up and lead and empower them to do so when necessary.

The evolution of followership serves as an unrecognized catalyst of the varied definitions of leadership throughout history. Over the past century, leadership has evolved from dominance to influence, innate natural and heroic abilities to behavioral characteristics, and a transferable process within groups. In tandem, followership has evolved from an act of submission, humility, and adaptability. It has transitioned to a voluntary acceptance and buy-in of a vision based on the capabilities and influence of a leader.

There are actual benefits that emerge from a positive leader/follower relationship. When leaders recognize the value of the follower and utilize strategies for communicating that value to the follower through engagement, effective leadership, trust and development, there is no limit to the potential of the leadership brand. I encourage you to strongly consider and embrace follower inclusion and maximize the valuable asset that leaders have in their followers. Next, let's take a look at some of the more useful strategies to communicate these new leadership lessons.

Chapter 9

WHAT ARE YOU COMMUNICATING?

"The art of communication is the language of leadership." [102] – James Humes

Effective communication is an art that is central to an effective leadership brand. One of the core elements of leadership is a leader's ability to communicate. The success of a vision often lies in the leader's ability or inability to convey their ideas and intentions. How will others understand your philosophies, vision, and strategies unless these elements are appropriately communicated and interpreted? As we continue our discussion on the value and inclusion of followers, understand that in order to influence, it is necessary to disseminate every message clearly using the appropriate communication tools. We will cover critical areas of communication such as understanding the communication cycle and the value of listening. We will also look at the types of messages that are critical to successful communication.

So how do you communicate? What do you communicate? Why is it necessary to communicate? The answers to these are all questions that eliminate barriers that hinder successful communication and effective leadership. Leaders with the inability to communicate, risk the possibility of adverse leadership outcomes and leadership brand perceptions. As simple as the idea of communicating may seem, doing so effectively can be challenging. You want your leadership brand to be known as one with clear and relevant messages that address related ideas.

Effective communication is the first step to impactful leadership. Viable, trustworthy, sustainable, and successful leadership brands, all include a well-communicated vision and strategy for the followers. If you think about it, how can followers help contribute toward someone else's vision or goal if they don't fully understand it themselves? Subsequently, how will leaders know if their message is understood without regular communication and feedback with their followers? Effective communication bridges this gap between leader and follower. It also helps others accurately interpret your leadership brand.

Communication is a key contributor to the functionality of a leader's vision.[103] It is also a necessary agent in the effort toward building a healthy leader/follower relationship. Communication is a connecting thread in developing relationships with everyone who is impacted by your brand. Understanding communication begins with understanding the measurement of whether or not communication between the leader and follower is working. It all begins with what I refer to as the communication cycle.

The Communication Cycle

Communication is the act of conveying information to create understanding.[104] Communication can be intentional, or it can be unintentional. It is also presented in various ways such as verbal or written communication, body language, and even silence. The most challenging aspect is that we all hope that our communication efforts are received as intended.

I believe that the communication process can be broken down into four aspects: the message, the transmitter, the receiver, and the interpretation. The message is the intended information that will be shared. The transmitter is the originator and disseminator of the message, while the receiver is the party who will receive the message. Lastly, the interpretation is the meaning of the message, as understood by the receiver. An important part of this process and the key measurement of effectiveness lies in the interpretation. The interpretation of the message must be the same as what the transmitter intended. The responsibility of the transmitter is to deliver the message as thoroughly as possible.

Just as with your leadership brand, communication alignment occurs when the intended message is communicated well and accurately interpreted. Ineffective communication occurs when the interpretation was inaccurate either due to the transmitter's inability to provide a clear and concise message or the receiver's erroneous or misguided interpretation. This philosophy is the same in any relationship whether leader to follower, parent to child, spouse to spouse, colleague to colleague, business to consumer or any other scenario that involves message transmission and interpretation. However, within a leadership branding context where one message is transmitted to numerous receivers, the task of properly communicating and achieving alignment is daunting.

Do you remember The Telephone Game that most of us played as children? The first person whispered a message and that message was passed from one person to another until the last person finally shared it with the group. I don't recall many times where the message that was shared was the same message from the beginning. This is how leadership communication becomes misinterpreted. Each time a message is transmitted, especially to multiple receivers, interpretation errors can potentially corrupt the accuracy of the original meaning.[105] Overcoming such barriers requires specific strategies that involve crafting specific types of messages, considering the audiences, communicating often, and engaging with the followers to receive feedback.

Earlier styles of leadership involved the role of the leader as the sole transmitter while followers demonstrated the role of the receiver. These instances of more authoritative, top-down leadership were customary, and followers had little input or limited opportunities to provide feedback. But when considering leadership communication, the roles of the transmitter and receiver are transferable, as are the roles of leader and follower. As a transmitter, the follower is now able to provide useful feedback and ideas of certain practices within the organization. Whereas historically, the follower possessed a somewhat limited voice within the organization.

Listening is another example of this leader/follower transference. While most leaders are accustomed to their role as transmitters of information, of equal value is their ability to also be the receivers of information. Doing so requires that leaders become active listeners as they receive information and feedback from their followers.

A critical and often overlooked aspect of communication is listening. Listening to feedback and engagement with followers helps leaders craft appropriate messages and respond accordingly to situations and inaccuracies that may arise. This approach also allows leaders to gain a better understanding of the most effective and ineffective strategies.

Leaders who listen create positive, trustworthy relationships and develop a mutual understanding with followers. Listening also yields many positive returns for the leadership brand such as:

1. gaining feedback that helps improve strategies;

2. understanding the followers' needs in order to address them; and

3. understanding the perceptions of your brand and the accuracy of your messages.

The most effective communicators are those who actively listen.[106]

Let's take a moment to explore active listening—the process of listening intentionally to those around you. Active listeners are better leaders. Leadership and listening are complementary. Active listening means listening with your entire body. It is listening first to understand; and then secondly, to be understood.[107] To actively listen, leaders should practice the following exercises:

1. **Listen to understand and not respond**. This means that instead of thinking of your response while the person is talking, you listen to them fully, observing all signals that will help you understand their perspective.

2. **Listen holistically.** Since only seven percent of a message is conveyed through words and the other 93 percent through non-verbal methods,[108] leaders must also pay attention to body language, expression, tone of written communication and verbal communication.[109]

Emotion and the context around the conversation also help with an accurate interpretation of the message.

3. **Avoid being defensive.** Active listening requires listening from a different perspective by removing opportunities to become defensive. To do so, listeners must take *self* out of the scenario, hold back the desire to provide a defense or rationale, and listen to seek clarity on the core meaning of what was said. This practice is especially important during tense, emotional, or difficult conversations. It will help drive the conversation toward understanding and resolution.

Let's talk more about this philosophy that leadership involves others. Consider this, your influence affects others, the results of your leadership affect others, every decision that you make directly affects someone else. When you realize that everything is not about you, you realize your potential impact and embrace feedback and even criticism as an opportunity for improvement. Listen and understand what others are trying to say and you will recognize that you are only a small factor in their scenario.

The last point to consider regarding listening is your response. Understand that your response to what you've heard should not be a rebuttal. As we discussed, part of your responsibility as a leader is to create an atmosphere that will allow others to thrive. That atmosphere must be inclusive of open and honest communication, which in turn builds trust. When followers trust their leader, there is a freedom to be more creative, empowered to provide more feedback, and motivation to continue working toward a common goal.

The ability to listen and decipher signals is a portal to a better understanding between the leader and the follower. Results of such knowledge ignite trust; which in turn leads to influence, impact, and a reputation of an effective leadership brand. Remember, less talk and more active listening is an equation that will improve your brand and help in communicating value to your followers.

Stability of Messaging

Communication is the gateway to connectivity. Effective communication creates lasting and sustainable impressions. However, ineffective communication, or a complete lack of communication, can potentially destroy progress and tarnish the leadership brand. The goal of effective communication is to create positive interpersonal connections coupled with aspirations and goals that align both individually and collectively.

The art of communication is imperative. Equally as important is determining what messages are the most relevant and impactful. Since we have established an understanding of how the communication process works, the next step in effective communication is for leaders to understand what messages are the most important to communicate. As you become more mindful of the flow of information that is communicated, you must begin to prioritize and categorize those messages.

Transparency is a necessary concept when building a trustworthy leadership brand. Transparency opens the lines of communication and demonstrates honesty.

Messages should not be vague, as that can cause speculation. Clear and transparent messages reduce the opportunity for misinterpretation, such as with the telephone game. Clear and transparent messages ensure that everyone is likeminded and aware of the brand's vision, mission, and intended culture.

When tailoring such messages, leaders should focus on:

1. Communicating Needs and Wants

2. Communicating the Vision

3. Communicating Follower Value

4. Communicating Emotional Intelligence

Targeted messaging that incorporates the communication cycle to help convey thoughts and solicit feedback will aid in maximizing opportunities for favorable outcomes.

Communicating Needs and Wants

Leaders and followers alike have both needs and wants. As you develop your leadership brand, it is important to communicate those needs and wants. Avoid allowing assumptions and inaccurate interpretations to govern the perception of your leadership brand. It is essential that you clearly communicate expectations concerning productivity, outcomes, job descriptions and other responsibilities, work ethic, organizational culture, and more.

Whatever the unique and specific areas of your leadership environment, communicate everything and communicate often. Communication establishes those standards that ensure that followers are clear on how to move forward. Doing so also raises followers' consciousness about goals while clarifying and aligning their own goals. This type of transparent communication eliminates the need and instinctual tendency for others to gather their own conclusions regarding your leadership desires.

Additionally, leaders should allow their followers to share their needs and wants.[110] Doing so eliminates misconceptions that could lead to perceived leadership inconsistencies. This allows for more effective transmitter and receiver roles as they also become interchangeable. Remember that one objective is to provide an impression of leadership stability and confidence. Confidence is enhanced with more knowledge and understanding of the perceptions and impressions of your followers. Confident leaders also develop confident followers.

Communicating the Vision

Leadership is a relationship. Although the leadership role may be perceived as isolated, its success and effectiveness rely on the participation and inclusion of the followers. The followers represent the environment in which leadership occurs. They are the laborers who operate at the heart of the vision. In many situations, followers are true representatives of a company because they are more visible than even the leader.

Considered followers as messengers of your leadership brand who communicate the vision to external audiences daily through their various roles and responsibilities. Thus, the leader must clearly communicate the vision and mission to ensure that the message is properly disseminated. If the receiver does not fully interpret the message or vision and miscommunicates it to others, the leadership brand is also miscommunicated.

Accurately communicating your mission and vision requires first that you are clear about it yourself. Think about your responsibility and accountability as a leader as well as your commitment to those impacted by your brand. Consider factors such as your code of ethics, leadership philosophies, values, and your *why,* and use those variables to develop an accurate representation of your brand.

As a leader, you must understand *why* you are leading. Your *why* is the source of your inspiration to lead and serves as motivation to continue. *New York Times* bestselling author Simon Sinek believes that great leaders inspire action when they first understand their *why*. *Why* do you want to lead? The *why* directly correlates to your vision and mission because it allows you to think about the contribution that you want to make (mission) and the impact that you hope to achieve (vision). When determining your *why,* consider the results of your leadership BRAND assessment, your personal attributes, and other distinguishing factors, and how those align to develop a mission and vision that represents your brand.

Communicating Follower Value

In the last chapter, we discussed the importance of valuing followers. This is possibly the most substantial message that a leader must consistently and genuinely communicate. In today's competitive workforce, individuals are no longer bound to a particular job. Studies show that millennials specifically are not loyal to their employers[111] and are likely to switch employers for various reasons easily. They value their comfort and leisure time and may be more likely to leave leaders who do not make them feel valued.

Although millennials may lead the charge in this behavior, they are not the only ones who understand their value as a follower. An increased number of employees understand the shift of leadership power that has transferred to the follower. They also understand the importance of their contributions. Disgruntled or underappreciated followers will seek new employment when experiencing a perceived lack of appreciation. Leaders who lack outward expressions of appreciation experience employee disloyalty, rapid turnover, low employee morale, and lack of productivity.

Studies have shown that leaders who communicate appreciation for their followers are more successful, have longer-lasting relationships, and experience higher employee morale. It is your decision as to the appropriate measures to take to show appreciation. However, communication is indeed important to establish this type of culture. Understanding this, the leader must establish an open and transparent line of organizational communication. The messages that are communicated positively impact the commitment, productivity, and morale of the follower.

Communicate Emotional Intelligence

A leader's level of emotional intelligence often determines the potential for effectiveness. Leaders with high emotional intelligence can appropriately interpret and manage emotions. This ability includes regulating their own emotions as well as adjusting to those of others. Such qualities are beneficial because they demonstrate the leader's ability to relate. In doing so, they are also able to influence their organizational culture.

High emotional intelligence improves the leader and follower relationship and team dynamics. Positive interactions increase when leaders can interpret the emotions of their team and address those signals accordingly. Analyzing emotions incorporates the art of active listening and using those skills to observe the tone of voice, body language, and the spoken and unspoken cues that serve as prompts for how one truly feels. Often, individuals suppress their feelings, especially within a team. In these cases, a leader's emotional intelligence helps break communications barriers and allows the leader to establish an open and trusting environment.

A lack of emotional intelligence makes the leader appear detached and self-centered, causing difficulty in trusting the leadership brand.[112] One remedy is that leaders exhibit great self-awareness.[113] There must be self-awareness of one's emotions and the potential impact of those emotions on those affected by the leadership brand. Self-aware leaders recognize and modify their emotions, control their impulses and moods, and self-regulate to achieve desired outcomes such as connecting with teams and stimulating emotional and intellectual growth.

There is a saying that "a team takes on the coach's personality," meaning that the leader's characteristics become the organization's persona. Followers take their emotional cues from the top.[114] Selfish leaders can generate selfish followers. Empathetic leaders create empathetic followers. Even in situations where leaders are not the most visible, their attitudes and characteristics have a trickledown effect on their teams. Take a moment to self-reflect and answer these questions: How would others rate your level of emotional intelligence? What factors contribute to this rating? What can you do to improve?

In line with emotional intelligence, the last and most compelling communication approach involves communicating emotion. Leaders must be believable in their delivery, whether written or verbal. For followers to capture the momentum needed to carry out the vision, leaders must communicate genuine and appropriate emotions.

When Steve Jobs took over as the CEO of Apple, he presented his followers with an exciting and innovative new form of technology. His conversations, marketing tactics, and products matched Apple's new brand that Jobs was creating. He communicated through example, as well as traditional communications methods, how he wanted others to feel about this product. The energy that he conveyed became the shared culture of the Apple organization.

Followers cannot buy-in if your emotion does not align with your message. Emotions are contagious, and none of the other communication tactics that we have discussed can be useful if leaders are not enthusiastic about their vision. Utilizing passion, body language, and energy when communicating with followers is key to transferring that same momentum and energy. As a leader, you must believe in your vision so that others will also. Using compelling stories, anecdotes, and creative communication methods are all impactful ways to generate buy-in.

Have you ever watched a leader participate in a press conference during a crisis, the launch of something new, or maybe even an interview? If so, you may recall the leader's actions, behaviors, and relatability. Did their emotions instill trust or likeability? Did the emotions align appropriately with the topic? How you communicate your feelings and reactions to a situation will either incite action and response or create distrust.

Strategic communication methods are valuable tools for building an impactful leadership brand. These strategies shape meaning, build trust, create a reputation, and develop relationships with your internal followers as well as external audiences.[115] Thinking through some of these best practices helps generate positive outcomes and develop loyal and committed followers who contribute positively to your leadership brand.

Chapter 10

CHANGING THE FUTURE

"Do not follow where the path may lead. Go instead where there is no path and leave a trail." [116] -Ralph Waldo Emerson

In our fast-paced, interconnected, and technologically advanced world, we sometimes find ourselves undergoing endless attempts to stay current. Not only is this a task in itself, but equally as daunting is staying ahead of our ever-changing world. In every aspect of life, there is a guarantee that some type of change will occur. Change is inevitable. If it has not yet occurred for you, it will. Your leadership brand should stand out as one that considers not only the now but also actively engages in plans for the future.

Change in itself is a sign of growth and evolution. [117] Despite the conditions surrounding change, those affected by it must make appropriate adjustments in order to succeed. Preparing and properly managing your leadership brand during change is mission critical. It requires flexibility and proactive strategies to transition properly from one dimension to the next. Constantly fighting to catch up, will guarantee that you are eventually left behind.

Your leadership brand will face change for various reasons. Yet even the most accepted and conventional motives for change require strategic thinking and specific planning. Preparing and adjusting to change reduces the possibility that your brand will be associated with chaos, disruption, or a lack of organization and strategy.

Change is the disruption of an identified culture. Though some resist and fear it, research suggests that change reflects the presence of growth and is necessary to achieve success and longevity. This is also true for your brand.

During our discussion of the Leadership BRAND Assessment in Chapter 7, we discussed the need to think ahead about the negatives and potential barriers affecting your brand. We discussed having a game plan for those barriers and being forward-thinking in your strategies to overcome them. The answers to that section of your assessment can serve as guides for future thinking and strategizing. Waiting to lead – or act – until a change occurs is too late. The present is the time to think ahead about the possibilities of the future; and develop your game plan of attack.

So, what will change? That's a loaded question because the possibilities are never-ending. Anything can change such as the way we communicate, to the way that we do business. Even the way we lead, can change. Think back to 20, 10, or even five years ago – as a matter of fact, think back one year ago. Many facets of our world are drastically different today. Around 20 years ago, people used what is now deemed *snail mail* – the traditional US Postal Service-- to deliver messages and documents. Today the post office is competing heavily to keep their doors open. Waiting two to three days for correspondence is an eternity in our instantaneous society.

The next wave of change included email. Yet even now, email is transitioning into a thing of the past. Today we have cloud-sharing, apps, and tools such as Skype, Facetime, and text messaging moving steadily to the forefront. Leaders who are not abreast of these and other types of changes will eventually become extinct. In contrast, leaders who are forward-thinking and plan for unexpected shifts will gain a competitive edge.

These are only small examples of the type of change that happens daily. Leaders must have the flexibility to anticipate and adjust quickly to evolving trends of all kinds. If not, they will find themselves as overshadowed and overlooked as the trend that they are stuck in.

Change can happen gradually or in an instant without warning. For example, the 9-11 terrorist attacks forever changed the way the world travels. Growing up near the airport, I went on outings just to watch the planes take off and land. We weren't going anywhere, only sitting at a gate watching the planes. Now, airports barely allow individuals to enter unless they are traveling. 9-11 also caused many security changes. I remember people being frustrated with the TSA workers because they had to throw away their liquids or remove their shoes. Now however, those actions are a new norm.

When thinking about the COVID-19 pandemic, change is an understatement. This pandemic completely disrupted the world as we knew it. Companies were forced to adjust quickly to changes that they never considered. As we discussed earlier, schools and universities rushed to develop plans to transition their students and staff to a virtual environment without compromising the integrity of their work and learning. Healthcare leaders revamped hospital visitation, triage, and the admission processes for the safety and protection of everyone. Restaurants, grocery stores, and other businesses had to quickly discover innovative ways to serve their customers. Those companies who were able to adjust survived, while those who were not prepared, closed, or suffered tremendously.

What's my point? Change happens, and whether they are ready, willing, and able-- or not, leaders must prepare. They should plan, adjust, and then readjust. They must be open to ideas that may seem radical or out of the box, and they must rely on input from their team members. Leaders cannot be afraid of change.

Thinking ahead and preparing beforehand is an excellent way to move quickly when times call for change. For example, in 2014, the City of Atlanta experienced extreme chaos when snow and ice covered the city unexpectedly within a matter of minutes. People were stranded in cars for hours, children slept at their schools overnight, and freeways quickly turned into parking lots. Additionally, most of the state remained closed for an unusually longer period than usual. Afterward, some businesses prepared and planned for similar future events.

I mentioned earlier about one school that developed an extensive inclement weather plan that was later used during the COVID shut down. Leaders of the school incorporated virtual learning strategies for future instances of prolonged closures due to inclement weather after the 2014 ice storm. They thought ahead and were prepared but never had to use the plan...until COVID-19. While others scrambled to find alternatives for the last-minute exodus from public spaces, this school had a contingency plan in place because they thought ahead. Although minor adjustments were inevitable, the transition was a lot smoother because leaders had the notion of planning ahead and preparing for future changes.

Future Smart Leaders

The ability to initiate change helps ensure your future as a leadership brand. Leaders much become future smart. Future smart is an intentional way of thinking about what's to come. Future smart leaders notice early warning signs of possible change and act accordingly based on possible solutions. They adopt a different worldview that looks at situations from a futuristic perspective. Later in this chapter, we will explore a three-step process that helps leaders develop a more future smart strategy.

If any leader hopes to survive in our present environment, innovation is a must.[118] Innovation does not just involve a creative idea, however. Innovation consists of thinking ahead, identifying intelligent solutions, and developing proactive strategies to predict and solve problems of the uncertain future.[119] Think of it this way, who would have thought it possible that the world would come to a halt in 2020? Who would have believed that newscasts would air from a reporter's home, that all students, from early to higher learning, would receive instruction virtually from home, and that people would not be able to gather in large crowds, would have to wear masks, and stay home for months? A future smart leader would at least come close.

Thinking ahead is really about foresight and vision. It is thinking about all of the possibilities and planning appropriately while knowing that there are no guarantees. Sound complicated? The truth is that we are all future thinkers in some capacity. Let's take a moment and do a little exercise.

Look at the phrases below and tally how many you have considered, spoken, and/or implemented throughout your life.

THINKING AHEAD	
"I need to plan ahead"	"One day I will…"
"My career goals involve…"	"My retirement"
"My 401K"	"My plans for the weekend"
"Saving for the college fund"	"I've set these goals"
"My dream car"	"My health insurance"
"Next year I plan to…	"My dream wedding"
"When I grow up…"	"My savings account"

How many of these futuristic phrases have you experienced or verbalized? Whether saving for a dream home or investing for retirement, the future remains a present-day discussion. The majority of these phrases are likely familiar, suggesting that, even though we may not realize it, the future is often at the forefronts of our minds. The next step is to dig deeper and stretch that thinking to develop possible solutions that shape the future and not just adjust to it.

Scenario Planning

We've discussed that leadership is based on implementing an unprecedented action that will lead to influence. In order to have impactful actions, it is practically a necessity that leaders not only think about the future, but actively plan for it. Doing so involves planning from the future back to the present.[120]

Of course, no one can accurately predict the future. However, anyone can plan for it. Your leadership brand cannot thrive without future planning. This type of planning enables you to anticipate future risks, as well as opportunities, while allowing time to plan and prepare.[121] To do this, the most comprehensive method that most accurately identifies these risks and opportunities is scenario planning.

Scenario planning is an aspect of a more intensive process known as strategic foresight. It is the process for developing potential solutions to potential future environments. In this case, it is planning for the future of your leadership environment by considering the many possible alternative futures and developing plans that explore approaches to those.[122]

Without moving too deeply into the theories of strategic foresight, scenario planning is a simpler alternative. Scenario planning functions as a guide to help you think about the potential future. The process stretches your thinking as a leader, sharpens and broaden your strategies, and helps identify key drivers and your leadership capabilities. Once you understand future possibilities, you can take the necessary steps to prepare your brand for those possibilities.

Scenarios are used to evaluate expected performance against differing options for the future. Scenario planning helps analyze a possible future scenario, or uncertainty while assessing your capacity and future potential of thriving based on possible solutions. This approach is especially beneficial for leaders developing strategic plans for the future.

Here's an example. At an early age, my daughter decided that she wants to be a surgeon when she grows up. She loves watching kid-friendly television shows that portray doctors and surgeries. While watching with her one day, I noticed that the portrayals did not show modern depictions of the medical environment. They showed surgeries in the more traditional sense such as doctors operating on patients with scalpels.

Today, most surgeries are conducted using robots. There are more and more surgical procedures happening with the use of robotic arms. Yes, the physicians are directing those arms, but they are doing so almost the same way that one would play a video game – with remote controls. By the time my daughter enters medical school, scalpels may be obsolete. In fact, how out of the box would it be to think that in the next 13 years, doctors may even be able to perform surgeries remotely from home?

Thinking about the possibility of remote surgery is an example of future thinking and scenario planning. We recognize that the way surgery is performed may change. We think about possible scenarios of what the future of surgeries might look like. We explore possible solutions and ways to thrive in the new potential environment.

The scenarios we envision and plan for are not just random ideas and suspicions. As the leader, take the time to research trends and study the appropriate fields to learn what inventions and possibilities exist. Of course, creating your own innovative solutions to these scenarios is welcome and will undoubtedly distinguish your brand as a leader in the field.

The next step is to determine what to do with this new information and discovery. In our example, once my husband and I realized that our daughter had not been exposed to accurate depictions of the medical environment that she will one day experience, we decided to let her join the Robotics Club. After all, robots are the future. This was a way to expose her early on to concepts that will soon become the new norm no matter what field she decides to study.

Leaders who are future thinkers must adopt this same model in order to remain relevant in the future. Remember these steps:

- Identify the problem or uncertainty.

- Explore future smart solutions.

- Engage and develop your understanding.

- Own and lead the future of the field.

Developing a Strategy

So how do we tie all of this together? When thinking about your leadership brand, remember that planning is critical to success and sustainability. You want to possess the ability to grow and thrive for years despite any changes. Leading the future means being strategic with a viable plan or strategy.

There are three major components to a future smart strategy. First, there is the *"why."* The why represents why we need a solution. It is possessing strategic foresight to help identify drivers of change, also known as *key drivers*.

Why did we need to learn robotics in the earlier example? Because the advanced technology in the medical field was a key driver of the change in surgeries of the future. Key drivers can be disruptions to the norm. Technological advances disrupted the standard or customary way of performing surgeries, replacing the human hand with the use of robots. Understanding the *why* means possessing the ability to look broadly and proactively at all options that could change and factors that will contribute to those changes.

The next aspect of strategic planning involves strategic thinking or the *how*. Here you will think about how to overcome those key drivers and barriers,[123] how to continue to meet your goals, and how your brand will thrive despite pending changes. As mentioned earlier, discovering possible solutions requires research and analysis about what is going on in your environment and how projected changes might look. The *how* heavily involves gaining insight.

The final step in developing your strategy involves strategic planning or the *what*. This is the phase in which you will create actionable plans.[124] These plans should be purposeful and intentional ways to achieve future goals. The *what* is the last step because the research and understanding of the issue must happen before a plan can be developed.

It is important to remember that your future smart solutions won't always seem realistic. In fact, in many cases, the more out of the box the solution may seem, the better. Centuries ago, it was probably not realistic to think that phones would have the ability to talk to us and give us information by a simple "hey!" prompt. It was also probably unrealistic to believe that entire meals could be cooked and even heated in a matter of seconds using this thing called a microwave! Some of our grandparents or even great grandparents may have a hard time grasping the concept that a document that once took a few days to deliver could be electronically transported to the recipient before finishing a sentence.

It is important to note that the future-thinking aspect of strategic planning is different from strategic planning in the more traditional sense. Traditional strategic planning helps you manage your goals, priorities, focus areas, and the overall short, medium, and long-term strategies that illustrate key aspects of your leadership brand. The traditional strategic plan is your internal diagram that pertains specifically to your brand.

There is one issue with strategic planning that excludes future thinking however. How can you develop long term goals and strategies if you have not considered what the future will look like in the long-term? Basing your long-term off of present circumstances will not yield beneficial results. One thing is certain; today's trends will not stay the same for long. Trends will only continue to change more rapidly.

Strategic foresight considers all of the factors outside of your internal conditions.[125] These external factors will help strengthen your strategic plan and prepare you more accurately for the future. You will incorporate strategies in your plan based on the other factors that you gathered and learned from your future thinking explorations.

Without future thinking and proper planning your leadership brand could potentially yield unrecoverable consequences when faced with the changes in trends and environment that the future holds. Taking unprecedented actions will set your leadership brand apart and set it up for longevity. In other words, foresight and intentional efforts to think ahead create a well-positioned, viable strategic plan for the future of your leadership brand.

Future planning is an important piece for defining your leadership brand scenario for many reasons. In addition to remaining abreast of future trends, it also helps you understand and plan for the unexpected. In the next chapter we will discuss navigation and preparation for the unpredictable pressures of leadership and how enduring those pressures is also a contributor to defining your leadership brand.

Chapter 11

LEADERSHIP RESILIENCE

"Uneasy lies the head that wears a crown." [126] - King Henry IV

You may wonder what lies ahead with a chapter entitled *Leadership Resilience*. My objective here is to move away from some of the principles and approaches to your leadership brand that we have discussed previously and use this final chapter to offer encouragement and motivation. I want to encourage you to continue through the challenges, uncertainties, and even the failures that impact your journey toward leadership.

Numerous antidotes address navigating the responsibilities and perks of leadership. There is an unaddressed facet of the personal leadership brand that is the polar opposite of those perks. This involves the not-so-glamorous side of leadership: the personal and professional challenges, isolation, failures, and roadblocks that are inevitable. While rarely discussed and often feared, this unpopular side of leadership, when faced courageously, often yields positive benefits.

Leadership is at times painful and uncomfortable. These experiences are personal because only you -- the leader – face them. Leaders must be courageous and exude perseverance especially during the times that are so overwhelming that they bear the potential to slow or halt your progress.

Before you achieve your leadership goals, the path to that point can present many challenges. Regardless of the pressure however, *endure the discomfort.* I would even venture to say, "Embrace the discomfort." On the other side of that discomfort comes the achievement of your goals, the lessons learned, and strength and development that you gained while enduring . Let's talk about this more!

Not many people look forward to discomfort. It is *uncomfortable* being uncomfortable; and we do not like that feeling. There are not many who enjoy feelings of anxiety, temptation, confusion, disorientation, unease, isolation, pressure, loss, or stress. I recognize that those are some pretty intense feelings; but they are also feelings that are prevalent at various points through life and the leadership journey. Truly effective leaders are ones who have the ability to thrive and withstand, even in the most adverse situations.[127] Leaders who are strongly resilient believe that it is worthwhile to struggle and endure in order to gain wisdom from their experiences.[128]

We *need* to be uncomfortable at times in order to progress. As a leader, the tough decisions that are uncomfortable to make, are usually the ones that yield the greatest success. We cannot live without discomfort. For example, though pain is uncomfortable, it is also the body's way of signaling to us that something is wrong and/or needs our action. Pain and discomfort can therefore be viewed as signs of a *need* to improve.

Pain in the breast, for instance, can be an indication of breast cancer. If there were no pain to signal a problem and the issue remains untreated, the result is potentially life-threatening. Likewise, body aches and fevers are typically indications of a cold or the flu. They are all signals that an action is needed in order to *improve* your health. Pain is what I often refer to as a necessary evil. It never feels good, but the results, after we overcome it, always lead to improvement.

Fitness experts refer to pain during workouts as *good pain.* Although it does not feel good, the results from enduring the pain and moving forward with your workout include increased muscle size, improved performance, and enhanced capabilities. As with muscle training, the pain and discomfort that we encounter as leaders are signs that improvement and positive results that are on the way, *if we endure.*

The same holds true for your success. We need to feel uneasy and disturbed at times. In those moments, we realize that some sort of necessary action needs to take place. To get past the present state, there has to be a push that motivates next steps. That push is, oftentimes uncomfortable. We cannot resist discomfort. Doing so causes us to miss potentially beneficial situations. The greatness that adversity breeds in us is lost when we choose to give up.

Think about this…. If we are always comfortable, would we ever be inspired to move forward and take an action? The comfort zone is a behavioral state that operates in an anxiety-neutral condition, using a limited set of behaviors to deliver a steady level of performances, usually without a sense of risk. [129] That sounds very safe and not very courageous. Comfort does not require a lot of effort. It requires a minimal amount of effort, expectation, and drive. That does not sound like characteristics of an impactful leader.

How many times have we avoided leaving a job because we were "comfortable?" You knew that you had outgrown the position, that there was no room to grow, or that you possessed more skills than what your employer recognized. But still, because you were comfortable, you did not move.

Our level of comfort can deter our opportunities for improvement. The irony is that comfort, though pleasurable, can be our biggest hindrance. Meanwhile, discomfort, as agonizing as it may be, can be our best ally.

There are many instances of anxiety disorders that plague individuals. While the more extreme levels of anxiety should be managed, studies suggest that anxiety improves performance once optimal – or balanced — levels are reached.[130] This means that even though anxiety is uncomfortable, enduring it to a certain degree can improve your outcomes. The question becomes whether you quit because you are uncomfortable, or do you face the challenge head on and prevail at the end? My vote is the latter, endure and prevail!

The world is filled with examples of leaders who have birthed fantastic ideas and started very successful businesses because they were pushed out of their comfort zones. Whether due to layoffs or ineffective leadership, stressful environments or some other level of discomfort, they were inspired to improve because discomfort pushed them. The same outcome applies to those who have conquered personal challenges. In the end, the lessons learned reap positive outcomes. If leadership is personal, as we have discussed, then the personal challenges that you face are also contributors to your leadership brand.

So, what's my point? *We need discomfort and uncomfortable situations for growth!* While no one seeks such obstacles, once they are present, we should not be afraid to face them confidently and courageously. Doing so allows us to complete the lessons that we are intended to learn and become better individuals and leaders as a result. Tough situations build the personal characteristics and the character that we need to lead, inspire, and succeed. The key is to persevere and push through until the end.

Jamaican-born entrepreneur and writer of this book's foreword, Wesley J. Hall, is an excellent example of the growth and accomplishment that results from perseverance and pushing through difficulties. Hall is one of Canada's most influential powerbrokers. He is the executive chairman and founder of Kingsdale Advisors, a leading shareholder services and advisory firm with offices located in Toronto and New York. Hall's company serves as a trusted strategic advisor to management and boards, covering everything from governance to crisis communications.[131] His leadership brand is undoubtedly powerful and impactful; and it is also well-respected among those who experience it.

Hall's leadership brand outcomes have proven to be impactful. His colleagues and business partners describe him as hardworking, fearless, well-respected, and tenacious, among other favorable attributes. His parents mention recognizing his potential for success during his teenage years based on his characteristics and drive. His late sister described him as her backbone, one who takes care of his family and works hard to make sure that they are all doing well; and his wife proudly boasts of the confidence that he exudes.

What could be the driving force behind Wes Hall, the person, business leader, and the brand? One word:

perseverance. Perseverance relates to how one responds to certain life events.[132] It is a quality that helps us overcome hardships and challenges when others allow those challenges to consume them. As you will learn momentarily, Hall faced many challenges throughout his life. However, he did not back down from those experiences. Hall allowed them to instead groom him into the leader that he has become.

Despite his success today, Hall was not always a powerful businessman. He admits that as a young boy in an impoverished area of St. Thomas, Jamaica, few would have imagined that he would be such an influential force. In his office, Hall keeps a photo of his small childhood home on his desk. He uses the picture as a reminder of his journey from past to present.

Hall grew up with his grandmother and siblings. He credits his entrepreneurial mindset and leadership philosophies to his grandmother, whom he calls the first entrepreneur he ever met. At a very young age, Hall assisted his grandmother as she worked in the fields planting and growing fruit to sell in order for her family to have money for their necessities. From that experience, he developed his work ethic. Hall describes his grandmother as industrious and hardworking. These adjectives are used by many to describe Hall today.

Hall is noted for his courage and fearless risk-taking. These attributes are vital for making lucrative business decisions required in his field. His fearlessness is also critical in his industry. That fearlessness has also led to the respect and admiration of other business colleagues who are inspired by his example. Hall's characteristics are pieces to his exemplary leadership brand customization. But how did he acquire them?

Hall attributes his courage to survival skills that he learned when he was forced to leave his grandmother's home and live in what became an abusive situation. After his last abusive encounter with his biological mother, he was put out of her home when he was 13 years old. For nearly two years, Hall lived on his own with no strategy for school, food, or shelter. He was later taken in by a foster family where he stayed for one year. At the age of 16, he was able to move to Canada to live with his father. The transition to a new country, family, school, and structured life was another uncomfortable scenario for Hall; but he endured. Thanks to his perseverance, the lessons that he gained from the troubled years yielded a return later.

Being on his own at such an early age taught Hall responsibility and strength. Despite his very dire circumstances, he persevered through those challenging times. His lessons from the past were vital to his ability to successfully overcome new challenges and obstacles. During his early adult years, Hall lost his brother tragically. The grief of that death took a toll on him, yet he continued to move forward, despite his pain. Research shows that those who display resilience during difficult situations tend to be more autonomous and independent.[133] Those who endure possess qualities that yield positive outcomes.

Hall's life has consisted of remarkable accomplishments over adversity, loss, poverty, and instability. However, he credits those experiences with molding him into the leader and person he is today. His leadership BRAND is derived from his beliefs, reactions, abilities, negatives in life, and distinctions that were all primarily influenced by his personal experiences, exposures, and lessons learned.

Whereas it would have been easier to give up many times, Hall persevered and used those life lessons to achieve his goals. His thirst for knowledge and achievement was exemplified by his father, who valued education and continuously challenged him to be successful.[134] His work ethic, tenacity, and drive to achieve were cultivated as he worked his way from a mailroom clerk to a business leader in the boardrooms of Bay Street—the financial capital of Canada. Though it was not an easy path, Hall was determined to overcome his challenges and thrive. Enduing the discomfort, despite the many odds that were against him, was key to his achievements.

Hall's leadership brand is not only successful, but it is tremendously influential and impactful. As we have noted before, although leadership is personal, the influence affects others. Likewise, the impact is far-reaching and can become so great that it exceeds even the leader's expectations. Once a leader has influenced others through the successful use of his/her leadership brand, the impact will begin to increase.

For example, Wes Hall's success on Bay Street has caused him to be sought out to lead some of the highest-profile deals and activist campaigns in North America, including billion-dollar mergers of top corporate companies. These are not his only leadership achievements, however. He is the owner of QM Environmental, a leading national environmental and industrial services provider with over 700 employees.[135] He also owns Titan Supply, a top manufacturer and distributor of rigging and wear products servicing industries in the oil and gas, construction, and transportation sectors.

Additionally, Hall is the owner of Harbor Club hotel, Curio Collection by Hilton- a premier resort, in St. Lucia. The influence and impact of his leadership brand on the island are undeniable. His staff buys-in to his leadership and speaks highly and admirably of Hall. Having met Hall and his team on his property in St. Lucia, I can attest that they genuinely appreciate his kindness, humility, compassion, and love for helping others. Remember what we discussed earlier, a team takes on the persona of its leader. This means that the reputation of the team is largely influenced by the leader. The best assessment of a leader's style is reflected in their team. Hall's team displays high morale, loyalty, excellence, and a commitment to the culture that he established. They exude qualities of the leadership brand that he demonstrates.

Whereas some may despise or overlook their challenges and the uncomfortable moments, Hall's experience growing up in an impoverished area of an island, motivated his desire to build the Harbor Club in St. Lucia. After witnessing the poverty and lack of jobs available on the island, he was compelled to not only build the resort, but to ensure that it operated locally. This creates more jobs for the people of the island. Enduring discomfort and allowing those lessons to positively shape him has strengthened Hall to become the leader he is today.

Research suggests that leadership orientation can be influenced by the psychological characteristics, cognitive biases, personality, and demographic characteristics of an individual.[136] All represent personal exposures, reactions, and environments that serve largely as contributors to leadership styles. The ability to endure, rather than quit in the face of temptation, serves as a catalyst for all that is to come. Leaders must persevere. They cannot give up; and they must not succumb to pressures and temptations.

I encourage you to allow your pending and future challenges to serve as motivational drivers throughout your leadership journey. Like Hall, challenges are often uncontrollable and can seem overwhelming; however, perseverance is the key. You must exude fortitude and courage to endure the uncomfortable times in order to experience the lessons learned and rewards that await at the finish line.

Building perseverance is similar to muscle training and analogous to the *good pain* that we described before. Though it is not a pleasurable experience, the more you work the perseverance muscle, the stronger you become. Look at your challenges as an indicator that the next level of growth and success is close. Each of the life lessons that Hall learned for instance, were inspired by some aspect of his life's journey. Most of these lessons were seemingly garnered during tougher times.

Personal values connect, shape, and derive from personal experiences.[137] The ability to endure challenges provides a deeper level of self-awareness and leads to a stronger and more authentic leadership brand. Your tenacity through challenges equips you to be unwavering in the face of future leadership challenges, temptations, and uncertainty. There is a connection between personal exposures and your leadership brand; and as with every aspect of your leadership, your tougher times can also lead to impact.

Leadership has tremendous benefits; however, it can be a lonely and isolated space for the individual charged with the role of leader. Do not let the discomfort of isolation and uncertainty stop you from pursuing your vision. Every circumstance builds a stronger leader. Do not let *"no,"* failures, or troubling paths halt the forward progression of your leadership actions. What sets your leadership brand apart is that you pursue and overcome difficulties. Take risks, continue moving forward, and do not back down, even when everything seems to work against you.

Remember, above all else, endure the discomfort and continue building that impactful leadership brand!

BIBLIOGRAPHY

"10 Examples of Powerful Global Branding" *The Logo Creative International Logo Design & Branding Studio*, September 3, 2019.

https://www.thelogocreative.co.uk/10-examples-of-powerful-global-branding/.

"Facebook Users by Country 2019." *Statista*. Accessed September 2019.

https://www.statista.com/statistics/268136/top-15-countries-based-on-number-of-facebook-users/

"Mark Zuckerberg." *Forbes Magazine*. Accessed October 19AD.

https://www.forbes.com/profile/mark-zuckerberg/#4a9252f73e06.

"The Atlanta Public Schools Cheating Scandal." Georgia Public Policy Foundation, July 2011.

https://www.georgiapolicy.org/issue/the-atlanta-public-schools-cheating-scandal/.

"U.S. Voter Turnout on Presidential Elections since 1908." *Statista,* n.d.

https://www.statista.com/statistics/262915/voter-turnout-in-the-us-presidential-elections/.

"Why the World Needs Ethical Leaders." SACAP, January 23, 2019.

https://www.sacap.edu.za/blog/coaching/ethical-leadership/.

Adamson, Allen. "Disney Knows It's Not Just Magic That Keeps a Brand on Top." *Forbes Magazine*, October 15, 2014.

https://www.forbes.com/sites/allenadamson/2014/10/15/disney-knows-its-not-just-magic-that-keeps-a-brand-on-top/#75aee3565b26.

Amvandenhurk. "PR Lessons from Build-A-Bear Pay Your Age Event." *Mind The Gap Public Relations*, October 10, 2018.

https://mindthegappr.com/pr-lessons-from-build-a-bear-pay-your-age-event/.

Anfara Jr., Vincent A., Pate, P. Elizabeth, Caskey, Micki M., Andrews, P. Gayle, Daniel, Larry G., Mertens, Steven B. and Muir, Mike. "Research Summary: Courageous, Collaborative Leadership." *National Middle School Association* (2008).

Astin, Helen S. "Leadership for Social Change." *About Campus* 1, no. 3 (1996): 4-10.

Avolio, Bruce J. and Gardner, William L. "Authentic Leadership Development: Getting to the Root of Positive

Forms of Leadership." *The Leadership Quarterly* 16, no. 3 (2005): 315-38.

Badenhausen, Kurt. "The World's Most Valuable Brands 2018." *Forbes Magazine*, May 22, 2019. https://www.forbes.com/sites/kurtbadenhausen/2018/05/23/the-worlds-most-valuable-brands-2018/#8b43e9b610c1.

Balmer, John M. T. "Strategic Corporate Brand Alignment: Perspectives from Identity Based Views of Corporate Brands." *European Journal of Marketing* 46, no. 7/8 (2012): 1064-92.

Bass, Bernard M., and Steidlmeier, Paul. "Ethics, Character, and Authentic Transformational Leadership Behavior." *The Leadership Quarterly* 10, no. 2 (1999): 181-217

Bass, Bernard M., and Stogdill, R. "Handbook of Leadership." *Theory, Research, and Managerial* (1981).

Bass, B.M. *Bass & Stogdill's Handbook of Leadership, 3rd Edition.* New York, NY: The Free Press, 1990.

Bass, Bernard. "The Inspirational Processes of Leadership." *Journal of Management Development* 7, no. 5 (1988): 21-31.

Bates, Suzanne. *Discover Your CEO Brand.* New York: McGraw-Hill Publishing, 2011.

Bauman, David C. "Evaluating Ethical Approaches to Crisis Leadership: Insights from Unintentional Harm Research." *Journal of Business Ethics* 98, no. 2 (2011): 281-95.

Bazerman, Max H. and Tenbrunsel, Ann E. "Ethical Breakdowns." *Harvard Business Review* 89, page 58-64.

Bell, Melissa. "Emmanuel Macron: From Political Novice to President." *Cable News Network*, May 7, 2017.

http://www.cnn.com/2017/04/20/europe/emmanuel-macron-french-election/.

Bennis, Warren G. *An Invented Life: Reflections on Leadership and Change*. MA: Addison Wesley Publishing Company, 1993.

Bennis, Warren. "The End of Leadership: Exemplary Leadership is Impossible without Full Inclusion, Initiatives, and Cooperation of Followers." *Organizational Dynamics* 28 (1): 71-79.

Bennis, Warren G., and Robert Townsend. *On Becoming A Leader, Vol. 36*. Reading, MA: Addison-Wesley, 1989.

Bezold, Clem. "Lessons from Using Scenarios for Strategic Foresight." *Technological Forecasting and Social Change* 77, no. 9 (2010): 1513-18.

Bianconi, Eva, Piovesan, Allison, Facchin, Federica, Beraudi, Alina, Casadei, Raffaella, Frabetti, Flavia, Vitale, Lorenza et al.

"An Estimation of the Number of Cells in the Human Body." *Annals of Human Biology* 40, no. 6 (2013): 463-71.

Bishop, William H. "Defining the Authenticity in Authentic Leadership." *The Journal of Values-Based Leadership* 6, no. 1 (2013): 7.

Boeker, W. (1997). "Strategic Change: The Influence of Managerial Characteristics and Organizational Growth." *Academy of Management Journal, 40*(1), 152-70.

Brizek, Michael G., Partlow, Charles G. and Nguyen, Lauren Ashley. "S. Truett Cathy: From Young Entrepreneur to a Foodservice Industry Leader." *Journal of Hospitality & Tourism Education* 19, no. 4 (2007): 7-10.

Breen, Jennifer Moss. "Leadership Resilience in a VUCA World." In *Visionary Leadership in a Turbulent World: Thriving in the New VUCA Context.* United Kingdom: Emerald Publishing Limited, 2017, 39-58.

Brown, I., Berry, P., Everard, et al. "Identifying Robust Response Options to Manage Environmental Change using an Ecosystem Approach: A Stress-Testing Case Study for the UK." *Environmental Science & Policy*, (2015) 52, 74-88.

Buehner Carl W., *What I Like About the Mormons: Carl W. Buehner 1965.* Brigham Young University Media Services, 1965.

Caldwell, C., Hayes, L. A., & Long, D. T. "Leadership, Trustworthiness, and Ethical Stewardship." *Journal of Business Ethics, 96*(4), 497-512.

Cameron, K. S., Dutton, J. E. and Quinn, R. E. "red. (2003), Positive organizational scholarship:

Cameron, Kim. "Responsible Leadership as Virtuous Leadership." in *Responsible Leadership*, Dordrecht: Springer, 2011, 25-35.

Carlton, Victoria. *Leadership in Action.* Melbourne: Melbourne University Press Digital, 2015.

Chermack, Thomas J. *Scenario Planning in Organizations.* San Francisco, CA: Berrett-Koehler Publishers, Inc., 2011.

Chou, Shih Yung. "Millennials in the Workplace: A Conceptual Analysis of Millennials' Leadership and Followership Styles." *International Journal of Human Resource Studies* 2, no. 2 (2012). 74.

Church, A.H. "What Do We Know About Developing Leadership Potential? The Role of OD in Strategic Talent Management." *OD Practitioner* (2014) 46 (3), 52-61.

Cook, Carly N., Sohail Inayatullah, Mark A. Burgman, William J. Sutherland, and Brendan A. Wintle. "Strategic Foresight: How Planning for the Unpredictable can Improve Environmental Decision-Making." *Trends in Ecology & Evolution* 29, no. 9 (2014): 531-41.

Coombs, W. Timothy. "Protecting Organization Reputations During a Crisis: The Development and Application of Situational Crisis Communication Theory." *Corporate Reputation Review* 10, no. 3 (2007): 163-76.

Cornish, E. (2004). *Futuring: The Exploration of the Future.* Maryland: World Future Society, 2004.

Coulson-Thomas, Colin. "Listening Leadership." *Effective Executive* 17, no. 3 (2014): 11-18.

Crant, J. Michael, and Bateman, Thomas S. "Charismatic Leadership Viewed from Above: The Impact of Proactive Personality." *Journal of Organizational Behavior* 21, no. 1 (2000): 63-75.

Crossan, Mary, Mazutis, Daina, Seijts, Gerard and Gandz, Jeffrey. "Developing Leadership Character in Business Programs." *Academy of Management Learning and Education* 12(2), 285-305.

da Silva Lopes, Teresa and Duguid, Paul, eds. *Trademarks, Brands, and Competitiveness.* Vol. 19. United Kingdom: Routledge, 2010.

Dadkhah, S., Bayat, R., Fazli, S., Einallah, K. T., & Ebrahimi, A. "Corporate Foresight: Developing a Process Model." *European Journal of Futures Research,* (2018) 6(1), 1-10.

Dalton, Matthew. "Emmanuel Macron Is Inaugurated as French President." *The Wall Street Journal*. Dow Jones & Company, May 14, 2017.

https://www.wsj.com/articles/emmanuel-macron-arrives-for-inauguration-as-french-president-1494750571

Daly, Alan J. "Rigid response in an Age of Accountability: The Potential of Leadership and Trust." *Educational Administration Quarterly* 45, no. 2 (2009): 168-216.

Davies, Barbara J. and Davies, Brent. "Strategic Leadership." *School of Leadership & Management* 24, no. 1 (2004): 29-38.

Derr, Cammi L. "Ethics and Leadership." *Journal of Leadership, Accountability and Ethics* 9, no. 6 (2012): 66-71.

Drucker, Chris. "Building Your Personal Brand." *Building Your Personal Brand* (podcast), n.d.

https://www.chrisducker.com/building-your-personal-brand/.

Fairhurst, Gail T. "Discursive Leadership: A Communication Alternative to Leadership Psychology." *Management Communication Quarterly* 21, no. 4 (2008): 510-21.

Fedesco, Heather Noel. "The Impact of (In)Effective Listening on Interpersonal Interactions." *International Journal of Listening* 29, no. 2 (2015): 103-6.

Felfe, Jörg, and Schyns, Birgit. "Followers' Personality and the Perception of Transformational Leadership: Further Evidence for the Similarity Hypothesis." *British Journal of Management* 21, no. 2 (2010): 393-410.

Finkelstein, Sydney, Cannella, Bert, Hambrick, Donald C. and Cannella, Albert A. *Strategic Leadership: Theory and Research on Executives, Top Management Teams, and Boards.* USA: Oxford University Press, 2009.

Gabriel, Yiannis. "The Caring Leader: What Followers Expect of Their Leaders and Why." *Leadership* 11, no. 3 (2015): 316-334.

George, Bill. *Authentic Leadership: Rediscovering the Secrets to Creating Lasting Value.* New Jersey: John Wiley & Sons, 2003.

Gini, Al, and Green, Ronald M. "Three Critical Characteristics of Leadership: Character, Stewardship, Experience." *Business & Society Review* (00453609) 119 (4): 435-46.

Graham, Jill W. "Servant-Leadership in Organizations: Inspirational and Moral." *The Leadership Quarterly* 2, no. 2 (1991): 105-19.

Grojean, Michael W., Resick, Christian J., Dickson, Marcus W. and Smith, D. Brent. "Leaders, Values, and Organizational Climate: Examining Leadership Strategies for Establishing an Organizational Climate Regarding Ethics." *Journal of Business Ethics* 55, no. 3 (2004): 223-41.

Halal, William E. "Leaders Who Listen: Authentic Leaders Care about What People Think." *Executive Excellence* 15 (1998): 12-13.

Hall, W. (2017). *WES | Wes Hall Documentary (Extended Version)*. YouTube. Available at:

https://www.youtube.com/watch?v=gdWqnEMx92I&t=1797 s.

Haller, Daniela K., Fischer, Peter and Frey, Dieter. "The Power of Good: A Leader's Personal Power as a Mediator of the Ethical Leadership-Follower Outcomes Link." *Frontiers in Psychology* 9 (2018): 1094.

Handrick, Laura. "25 Core Value Statements from 2018's Top Organizations." *Fit Small Business*, May 2018.

https://fitsmallbusiness.com/core-values-list/.

Hargrove, Erwin C. *Jimmy Carter as President: Leadership and the Politics of the Public Good*. Louisiana: LSU Press, 1999.

Hazy, James K. "Parsing the 'Influential Increment' in the Language of Complexity: Uncovering the Systemic Mechanisms of Leadership Influence." *International Journal of Complexity in Leadership and Management* 1, no. 2 (2011): 164-91.

Healy, Paul M., and Palepu, Krishna G. "The Fall of Enron." *Journal of Economic Perspectives* 17, no. 2 (2003): 3-26.

Herman, Roger E. "A Leadership Evolution." *Employment Relations Today* 26, no. 4 (2000): 73.

Hersh, E. (n.d.). "Using Effective Listening to Improve Leadership in Environmental Health and Safety." [online] *Executive and Continuing Professional Education.* Available at: https://www.hsph.harvard.edu/ecpe/listening-to-improve-leadership/.

Higgs, Malcolm, and Deborah Rowland. "Emperors with Clothes On: The Role of Self-Awareness in Developing Effective Change Leadership." *Journal of Change Management* 10, no. 4 (2010): 369-85.

Hilton, Steve. "The Social Value of Brands." *Brands and Branding* (2003): 47-64.

Horth, David Magellan and Vehar, Jonathan. "Becoming a Leader Who Fosters Innovation." *New York*, (2012), 1-25.

House, Robert J. "A Theory of Charismatic Leadership." *Leadership: The Cutting Edge.* Illinois: Southern Illinois University Press, 1977.

Hudson, Sara. "Overcoming Adversity" The Center for Independent Studies, 32, no. 3 (Spring 2016): 54–7.

Hunter, James C. *The World's Most Powerful Leadership Principle: How to Become a Servant Leader.* New York, Crown Business, 2004.

Ilies, Remus, Morgeson, Frederick P. and Nahrgang, Jennifer D. "Authentic Leadership and Eudaemonic Well-Being: Understanding Leader–Follower Outcomes." *The Leadership Quarterly* 16, no. 3 (2005): 373.

Itzhaky, Haya and York, Alan S. "Leadership Competence and Political Control: The Influential Factors." *Journal of Community Psychology* 31, no. 4 (2003): 371-81.

Jenkins, Helen M. "Ethical Dimensions of Leadership in Community Health Nursing." *Journal of Community Health Nursing* 6, no. 2 (1989): 103-12.

Jensen, S. M., & Luthans, F. "Entrepreneurs as Authentic Leaders: Impact on Employees' Attitudes." *Leadership & Organization Development Journal, 27*(8), 646-66.

Jones, Ian W. and Pollitt, Michael G. "Ethical and Unethical Competition: Establishing the Rules of Engagement." *Long Range Planning* 31, no. 5 (1998): 703-10.

Katz, James, Barris, Michael, and Jain, Anshul. *The Social Media President: Barack Obama and the Politics of Digital Engagement,* New York: Springer, 2013.

Kavathatzopoulos, Iordanis. "Leaders as Philosophers." *EBEN 2011.* Universiteit Antwerpen, 2011.

Khedher, Manel. "Personal Branding Phenomenon." *International Journal of Information, Business and Management* 6, no. 2 (2014): 29.

King James Bible. Nashville, TN: Holman Bible Publishers, 1973.

Kingsdale, A. (2019). *Kingsdale Advisors*. [website] Kingsdaleadvisors.com. Available at:

http://www.kingsdaleadvisors.com.

Kirkpatrick, S. A. and Locke, E. A. (1991). "Leadership: Do Traits Matter?" *The Executive*, (1991) 5(2), 48.

Kouzes, James M. and Posner, Barry Z. "*The Five Practices of Exemplary Leadership*." San Francisco: Wiley Publishers, 2003.

Kouzes, James M., and Posner, Barry Z. "Ethical Leaders: An Essay about Being in Love." *Journal of Business Ethics* 11, no. 5-6 (1992): 479-84.

Kouzes, J. M., & Posner, B. Z. *The Leadership Challenge, Vol. 3*. New York: John Wiley & Sons, 2006.

Kraemer, William J. and Barry A. Spiering. "Skeletal Muscle Physiology: Plasticity and Responses to Exercise." *Hormone Research in Pediatrics* 66(1): 2-16.

Kutler, Stanley I. *The Wars of Watergate: The Last Crisis of Richard Nixon*. New York: WW Norton & Company, 1992.

Lambert, Wendy Ecklund, Miears, Larry D., Anderson, Kelly Preston, Irving, Justin A., Iken, Stacie L., Krebs, Kristen D., Arfsten, Debra J., and Cater III, John James. "Servant Leadership Qualities of Principals, Organizational Climate, and Student Achievement: A Correlational Study." *Nova Southeastern University,* 2006, 1191.

Lindgren, M., & Bandhold, H. (2003). *Scenario Planning.* New York: Palgrave, 2003.

Lee, Sang M., and Silvana, Trimi. "Innovation for Creating a Smart Future." *Journal of Innovation & Knowledge* 3, no. 1 (2018): 1-8.

Lester. "LoveBeyondWalls." *LoveBeyondWalls.* Accessed October 19, 2019. http://www.lovebeyondwalls.org/.

Lord, Robert G., and Brown, Douglas J. "Leadership, Values, and Subordinate Self-Concepts." *The Leadership Quarterly* 12, no. 2 (2001): 133-152.

Lunenburg, Fred C. "Power and Leadership: An Influence Process." *International Journal of Management, Business, and Administration* 15, no. 1 (2012): 1-9.

Maccoby, Michael. "Why People Follow the Leader: The Power of Transference." *Harvard Business Review* 82, no. 9 (2004): 76-85.

MacKie, Doug. "13 Strength-Based Leadership and Team Coaching in Asia Pacific." *Coaching and Mentoring in the Asia Pacific* (2017), 127-133.

Maddi, Salvatore R., and Deborah M. Khoshaba. "Hardiness Training for Resiliency and Leadership." *Promoting Capabilities to Manage Post-Traumatic Stress: Perspectives on Resilience* (2003): 43-58.

Magellan, David Horth and Vehar, Jonathan. "Becoming a Leader Who Fosters Innovation." *Center for Creative Leadership* (2012), 4.

Maier, Craig T. "Weathering the Storm: Hauser's Vernacular Voices, Public Relations and the Roman Catholic Church's Sexual Abuse Scandal." *Public Relations Review* 31, no. 2 (2005): 219-27.

Marsh, N., McAllum, M., & Purcell, D. *Strategic Foresight: The Power of Standing in the Future.* Melbourne: Crown Content, 2002, 2.

Marzano, Giuseppe and Scott, N. R. "Consistency in Destination Branding: The Impact of Events." *Proceedings from Global Events Congress*, (2006): 196-205.

Mastrangelo, Angelo, Eddy, Erik R. and Lorenzet, Steven J. "The Importance of Personal and Professional Leadership." *Leadership & Organization Development Journal* 25, no. 5 (2004): 435-51.

MacDonald, Ronald R. "Uneasy Lies: Language and History in Shakespeare's Lancastrian Tetralogy." *Shakespeare Quarterly* 35, no. 1 (1984): 22-39.

McLaughlin, Jerry. "What Is a Brand, Anyway?" *Forbes Magazine*, January 9, 2012.

https://www.forbes.com/sites/jerrymclaughlin/2011/12/21/what-is-a-brand-anyway/#5df055aa2a1b.

Metcalf, Louise and Benn, Sue. "Leadership for Sustainability: An Evolution of Leadership Ability." *Journal of Business Ethics*112, no. 3 (2013): 369-84.

Miller, Beth Armknecht. "Building Your Leadership Brand." *Leadership*. Accessed May 2014.

https://www.thinkhdi.com/library/supportworld/2014/leadership-brand.aspx.

Montoya, Peter, and Vandehey, Tim. *The Brand Called You: Create a Personal Brand That Wins Attention and Grows Your Business*. New York: McGraw-Hill, 2009.

Moore, James H., and Wang, Zhongming. "Mentoring Top Leadership Promotes Organizational Innovativeness through Psychological Safety and is Moderated by Cognitive Adaptability." *Frontiers in Psychology* 8 (2017): 318.

Moore Johnson, Susan and Donaldson, Morgaen L. "Overcoming the Obstacles to Leadership." *Educational Leadership* 65, no. 1 (2007): 8-13.

Morris, Aldon D. and Staggenborg, Suzanne. "Leadership in Social Movements." *The Blackwell Companion to Social Movements* (2004): 171-96.

Muna, Farid A., and Ned Mansour. "Balancing Work and Personal Life: The Leader as Acrobat." *Journal of Management Development 28,* no. 2 (2009): 121-33.

Neubert, Mitchell J., Carlson, Kacmar, Dawn S., Roberts, James A. and Chonko, Lawrence B. "The Virtuous Influence of Ethical Leadership Behavior: Evidence from the Field." *Journal of Business Ethics* 90, no. 2 (2009): 157-70.

Nienaber, Ann-Marie, Hofeditz, Marcel and Romeike, Philipp Daniel. "Vulnerability and Trust in Leader-Follower Relationships." *Personnel Review* 44, no. 4 (2015): 567-91.

Northouse, Peter G. *Leadership: Theory and Practice.* Thousand Oaks, CA: SAGE Publications, Inc., 2013.

Norwood, Kathryn. "A Principal: The Power of Strengths-Based Leadership." *Educational Horizons* 83, no. 3 (2005): 204-6.

Ofori, George. "Leadership for Future Construction Industry: Agenda for Authentic Leadership." *International Journal of Project Management* 26, no. 6 (2008): 620-30.

Othman, Zaleba and Rahman, Rashidah Abdul. "Attributes of Ethical Leadership in Leading Good Governance." *International Journal of Business and Society* 15, no. 2 (2014): 359.

Palanski, Michael E., and Yammarino, Francis J. "Integrity and Leadership: Clearing the Conceptual Confusion." *European Management Journal* 25, no. 3 (2007): 171-84.

Pless, N. M. "Understanding Responsible Leadership: Role Identity and Motivational Drivers." *Journal of Business Ethics* (2007) 74, 437-56.

Porath, C. "Half of Employees Don't Feel Respected by their Bosses." *Harvard Business Review* 92 (2014)

Rampersad, Hubert K. *Authentic Personal Branding: A New Blueprint for Building and Aligning a Powerful Leadership Brand.* North Carolina: IAP, 2009.

Rath, Tom and Conchie, Barry. *Strengths Based Leadership: Great Leaders, Teams, and Why People Follow.* New York: Simon and Schuster, 2008.

Raford, Noah. "Online Foresight Platforms: Evidence for their Impact on Scenario Planning & Strategic Foresight." *Technological Forecasting and Social Change* 97 (2015): 65-76.

Resnick, Sheilagh, Ranis Cheng, Mary, Simpson, Mike and Lourenço, Fernando. "Marketing in SMEs: A "4Ps" Self-

Branding Model." *International Journal of Entrepreneurial Behavior & Research* 22, no. 1 (2016): 155-74.

Reynolds, J. Gregory, and Warfield, Walter H. "Discerning the Differences Between Managers and Leaders." *The Education Digest* 75, no. 7 (2010): 61.

Robertson, Melva. *Congratulations! It's a Brand: The Entrepreneur's Guide to Birthing the Brand, Increasing Visibility, and Identifying Your Target Audience.* Georgia: Create Space, 2016.

Russell, Robert F. "The Role of Values in Servant Leadership." *Leadership & Organization Development Journal* 22, no. 2 (2001): 76-84.

Schoemaker, Paul JH. "Scenario Planning: A Tool for Strategic Thinking." *Sloan Management Review* 36, no. 2 (1995): 25-50.

Seely, Taylor. "Build-a-Bear CEO Apologizes for 'Pay Your Age' Sale Fail." *USA Today,* July 13, 2018.

https://www.usatoday.com/story/life/allthemoms/2018/07/13/build-bear-ceo-apologies-failed-pay-your-age-sale/782550002/.

Selsky, John W. and Smith, Anthony E. "Community Entrepreneurship: A Framework for Social Change Leadership." *The Leadership Quarterly* 5, no. 3-4 (1994): 277-96.

Sezer, Ovul, Gino, Francesca, and Bazerman, Max H. "Ethical Blind Spots: Explaining Unintentional Unethical Behavior." *Current Opinion in Psychology* 6 (2015): 77-81.

Shandley, Thomas C. "The Use of Mentors for Leadership Development." *NASPA journal* 27, no. 1 (1989): 59-66.

Simmons, Richard. "Leadership and Listening: The Reception of User Voice in Today's Public Services." *Social Policy & Administration* 45, no. 5 (2011): 539-68.

Smallwood, Norm. "Define Your Personal Leadership Brand in Five Steps." *Harvard Business Review*, July 23, 2014. https://hbr.org/2010/03/define-your-personal-leadership).

Smeltzer, Larry R. "An Analysis of Receivers' Reactions to Electronically Mediated Communication." *The Journal of Business Communication (1973)* 23, no. 4 (1986): 37-54

Stillion Southard, Bjorn F., and Andrew D. Wolvin. "Jimmy Carter: A Case Study in Listening Leadership." *The International Journal of Listening* 23, no. 2 (2009): 141-52.

Stogdill, Ralph M. *Handbook of Leadership: A Survey of Theory and Research*. New York: Free Press, 1974.

Tenelshof, J. (1999). "Encouraging the Character Formation of Future Christian Leaders." *Journal-Evangelical Theological Society*, 42, 77-90.

Thomas, Anisya S., and Ramaswamy, Kannan. "Matching Managers to Strategy: Further Tests of the Miles and Snow Typology." *British Journal of Management* 7, no. 3 (1996): 247-61.

Thornton, James S. "Pain Relief for Acute Soft-Tissue Injuries." *Physician and Sportsmedicine* 25, no. 10 (1997): 108-14.

Tichy, Noel M. and Ulrich, David O. "SMR Forum: The Leadership Challenge -- A Call for the Transformational Leader." *Sloan Management Review (pre-1986)* 26, no. 1 (1984): 59.

Tilley, Catherine. "Built-in Branding: How to Engineer a Leadership Brand." Journal of Marketing Management 15, no. 1-3 (1999): 181-91.

Tucker, Bruce A. and Russell, Robert F. "The Influence of the Transformational Leader." *Journal of Leadership & Organizational Studies* 10, no. 4 (2004): 103-11.

Ulrich, Dave and Smallwood, Norm. *Aligning Firm, Leadership, and Personal Brand. Leader to Leader* New Jersey: Wiley Publishing, 2008.

Ulrich, Dave and Smallwood, Norm. "Building a Leadership Brand." *Harvard Business Review* 85, no. 7/8 (2007): 92.

Urbany, Joel E. "Inspiration and Cynicism in Values Statements." *Journal of Business Ethics* 62, no. 2 (2005): 169-82.

Verbos, Amy Klemm, Gerard, Joseph A. Forshey, Paul R., Harding, Charles S. and. Miller, Janice S. "The Positive Ethical Organization: Enacting a Living Code of Ethics and Ethical Organizational Identity." *Journal of Business Ethics* 76, no. 1 (2007): 17-33.

Walsh, J. P., Weber, K., and Margolis, J. D. "Social Issues and Management: Our Lost Cause Found." *Journal of Management,* (2003) 29, 859-81.

Watton, Emma, Lichtenstein, Scott and Aitken, Paul. "'Won't Get Fooled Again': How Personal Values Shape Leadership Purpose, Behavior and Legacy." *Journal of Management & Organization* (2019): 1-16.

Weick, K. E. and Sutcliffe, K. M. *Managing the Unexpected Assuring High Performance in an Age of Complexity.* San Francisco: Josey-Bass, 2001.

Williams, Joshua H. "Personality Styles That Influence Organizational Safety." In *ASSE Professional Development Conference and Exposition.* American Society of Safety Engineers, 2002, 1-11.

White, Alasdair. *From Comfort Zone to Performance Management*. Baisy-Thy, England: White & MacLean Publishing, 2009.

Winston, B.E., and Stone, A.G. "Leadership Talks." *School of Leadership Studies, Regent University,* Virginia Beach, VA 23464 - Leadership & Ethics. Regent University. https://www.regent.edu/acad/global/leadershiptalks/archive/jan_08_winston_stone.htm.

Young, Jon, and Firmin, Michael W. "Qualitative Perspectives Toward Relational Connection in Pastoral Ministry." *The Qualitative Report* 19 (2014): 1.

End Notes

[1] Emma Watton, Scott Lichtenstein, and Paul Aitken. "'Won't Get Fooled Again': How Personal Values Shape Leadership Purpose, Behavior and Legacy." *Journal of Management & Organization* (2019): 414.

[2] Michael Maccoby. "Why People Follow the Leader: The Power of Transference." *Harvard Business Review* 82, no. 9 (2004): 77.

[3] J. Gregory Reynolds and Walter H. Warfield. "Discerning the Differences Between Managers and Leaders." *The Education Digest* 75, no. 7 (2010): 61.

[4] Melva Robertson. *Congratulations! It's a Brand: The Entrepreneur's Guide to Birthing the Brand, Increasing Visibility, and Identifying Your Target Audience.* (Atlanta: Create Space, 2015): page 2.

[5] Bernard M. Bass and R. Stogdill. "Handbook of Leadership." *Theory, Research, and Managerial* (New Yorks, Free Press, 1981): 28.

[6] Daniela K. Haller, Peter Fischer, and Dieter Frey. "The Power of Good: A Leader's Personal Power as a Mediator of the Ethical Leadership-Follower Outcomes Link." *Frontiers in Psychology* 9 (2018): 1094.

[7] K. S. Cameron, J. E. Dutton, and R. E. Quinn. "red. (2003), Positive Organizational Scholarship: Foundations of a New Discipline."

[8] Daniela K. Haller, Peter Fischer and Dieter Frey. "The Power of Good: A Leader's Personal Power as a Mediator of the Ethical Leadership-Follower Outcomes Link." *Frontiers in Psychology* 9 (2018): 1064.

[9] Angelo Mastrangelo, Erik R. Eddy, and Steven J. Lorenzet. "The Importance of Personal and Professional Leadership." *Leadership & Organization Development Journal* 25, no. 5 (2004): 435.

[10] Roger E. Herman. "A Leadership Evolution." *Employment Relations Today* 26, no. 4 (2000): 73.

[11] J. M. Kouzes, and B. Z. Posner. *The Leadership Challenge, Vol. 3.* (New Jersey: John Wiley & Sons, 2006), 277.

[12] George Ofori. "Leadership for Future Construction Industry: Agenda for Authentic Leadership." *International Journal of Project Management* 26, no. 6 (2008): page 621.

[13] Ofori, "Leadership for Future," 625.

[14] Bill George. *Authentic leadership: Rediscovering the Secrets to Creating Lasting Value.* (New Jersey: John Wiley & Sons, 2003), 12.

[15] Melissa Bell. "Emmanuel Macron: From Political Novice to President." *Cable News Network*, May 7, 2017.

http://www.cnn.com/2017/04/20/europe/emmanuel-macron-french-election/.

[16] Matthew Dalton. "Emmanuel Macron Is Inaugurated as French President." *The Wall Street Journal.* Dow Jones & Company, May 14, 2017. https://www.wsj.com/articles/emmanuel-macron-arrives-for-inauguration-as-french-president-1494750571

[17] Cameron et al, "Positive Organizational Scholarship," 2.

[18] James Katz, Michael Barris, and Anshul Jain. *The Social Media President: Barack Obama and the Politics of Digital Engagement.* (New York: Springer, 2013), 215.

[19] Katz, *The Social Media President*, 215.

[20] Wendy Ecklund Lambert, Larry D. Miears, Kelly Preston Anderson, Justin A. Irving, Stacie L. Iken, Kristen D. Krebs, Debra J. Arfsten, and John James Cater III. Servant Leadership Qualities of Principals, Organizational Climate, and Student Achievement: A Correlational Study. *Nova Southeastern University*; 2006, 1191.

[21] Al Gini and Ronald M. Green. "Three Critical Characteristics of Leadership: Character, Stewardship, Experience." *Business & Society Review* (00453609) 119 (4): 441.

[22] Lambert, et al. *Servant Leadership Qualities of Principals, Organizational Climate, and Student Achievement*, 1191.

[23] Warren G. Bennis and Robert Townsend. *On Becoming A Leader. Vol. 36.* (Reading, MA: Addison-Wesley, 1989), 7.

[24] Sheilagh Resnick, Mary Cheng Ranis, Mike Simpson, and Fernando Lourenço. "Marketing in SMEs: A "4Ps" Self-Branding Model." *International Journal of Entrepreneurial Behavior & Research* 22, no. 1 (2016): 157.

[25] Hubert K. Rampersad,. *Authentic Personal Branding: A New Blueprint for Building and Aligning a Powerful Leadership Brand.* IAP, 2009. P, xiii

[26] Blog: http://www.valuing-your-talent-framework.com/sites/default/files/resources/THK-032%20John%20Adair.pdf

[27] Chris Drucker. "Building Your Personal Brand." *Building Your Personal Brand* (podcast), n.d. https://www.chrisducker.com/building-your-personal-brand/.

[28] Melva Robertson. *Congratulations! It's a Brand: The Entrepreneur's Guide to Birthing the Brand, Increasing Visibility, and Identifying Your Target Audience (Georgia: Create Space,* 2015): 20.

[29] "10 Examples of Powerful Global Branding" *The Logo Creative | International Logo Design & Branding Studio,* September 3, 2019. https://www.thelogocreative.co.uk/10-examples-of-powerful-global-branding/.

[30] Beth Armknecht Miller. "Building Your Leadership Brand." *Leadership.* Accessed May 2014.

https://www.thinkhdi.com/library/supportworld/2014/leaders hip-brand.aspx.

[31] Carl W. Buehner, *What I Like About the Mormons: Carl W. Buehner 1965*. Brigham Young University Media Services, 1965.

[32] Robertson, *Congratulations,* 89.

[33] John M. T. Balmer. "Strategic Corporate Brand Alignment: Perspectives from Identity Based Views of Corporate Brands." *European Journal of Marketing* 46, no. 7/8 (2012): 1065.

[34] Giuseppe Marzano and N. R. Scott. "Consistency in Destination Branding: The Impact of Events." *Global Events Congress*, (2006):196.

[35] Norm Ulrich and Dave Smallwood. "Building a Leadership Brand," *Harvard Business Review*, August 1, 2014. https://hbr.org/2007/07/building-a-leadership-brand.

[36] Peter Montoya and Tim Vandehey. *The Brand Called You: Create a Personal Brand That Wins Attention and Grows Your Business.* (New York: McGraw-Hill, 2009): 378.

[37] Rampersad. *Authentic Personal Branding,"* xiii.

[38] Rampersad, *Authentic Personal Branding,* 4.

[39] Norm Smallwood. "Define Your Personal Leadership Brand in Five Steps." *Harvard Business Review*, July 23, 2014. https://hbr.org/2010/03/define-your-personal-leadership).

[40] Rampersad, *Authentic Personal Branding*, 8.

[41] *King James Bible*. (Nashville, TN: Holman Bible Publishers, 1973), online.

[42] Kouzes and Posner, *The Leadership Challenge*, 3.

[43] "U.S. Voter Turnout on Presidential Elections since 1908." *Statista,*n.d. https://www.statista.com/statistics/262915/voter-turnout-in-the-us-presidential-elections/.

[44] "U.S. Voter Turnout on Presidential Elections since 1908." *Statista,*n.d.

[45] William H. Bishop. "Defining the Authenticity in Authentic Leadership." *The Journal of Values-Based Leadership* 6, no. 1 (2013): 7.

[46] Bishop. "Defining the Authenticity in Authentic Leadership." 7.

[47] Thomas C. Shandley. "The Use of Mentors for Leadership Development." *NASPA journal* 27, no. 1 (1989): 60.

[48] James H. Moore and Zhongming Wang. "Mentoring Top Leadership Promotes Organizational Innovativeness through Psychological Safety and is Moderated by Cognitive Adaptability." *Frontiers in Psychology* 8 (2017): 318.

[49] Ovul Sezer, Francesca Gino, and Max H. Bazerman. "Ethical Blind Spots: Explaining Unintentional Unethical Behavior." *Current Opinion in Psychology* 6 (2015): 77.

[50] Palanski, Michael E., and Francis J. Yammarino. "Integrity and Leadership: Clearing the Conceptual Confusion." *European Management Journal* 25, no. 3 (2007): 171.

[51] B.E. Winston and A.G. Stone. "Leadership Talks: Leadership and Ethics." *School of Leadership Studies*, Regent University, Virginia Beach, VA 23464 https://www.regent.edu/acad/global/leadershiptalks/archive/jan_08_winston_stone.htm.

[52] Sezer, Gino, and Bazerman. "Ethical Blind Spots," 77.

[53] Amy Klemm Verbos, Joseph A. Gerard, Paul R. Forshey, Charles S. Harding, and Janice S. Miller. "The Positive Ethical Organization: Enacting a Living Code of Ethics and Ethical Organizational Identity." *Journal of Business Ethics* 76, no. 1 (2007): 18.

[54] Cammi L. Derr. "Ethics and Leadership." *Journal of Leadership, Accountability and Ethics* 9, no. 6 (2012): 66.

[55] Bernard M. Bass and Paul Steidlmeier. "Ethics, Character, and Authentic Transformational Leadership Behavior." *The Leadership Quarterly* 10, no. 2 (1999): 6.

[56] Victoria Carlton. *Leadership in Action*. (Melbourne: Melbourne University Press Digital, 2015), 11.

[57] S. A. Kirkpatrick and E. A. Locke. "Leadership: Do traits matter?" *The Executive*, (1991) 5(2), 48.

58 Zaleba Othman and Rashidah Abdul Rahman. "Attributes of Ethical Leadership in Leading Good Governance." *International Journal of Business and Society* 15, no. 2 (2014): 359.

59 Laura Handrick. "25 Core Value Statements from 2018's Top Organizations." *Fit Small Business*, May 2018. https://fitsmallbusiness.com/core-values-list/.

60 Handrick, "25 Core Value Statements," 1.

61 Handrick, "25 Core Value Statements," 1.

62 "Why the World Needs Ethical Leaders." SACAP, January 23, 2019. https://www.sacap.edu.za/blog/coaching/ethical-leadership/.

63 Remus Ilies, Frederick P. Morgeson, and Jennifer D. Nahrgang. "Authentic Leadership and Eudaemonic Well-Being: Understanding Leader–Follower Outcomes." *The Leadership Quarterly* 16, no. 3 (2005): 373.

64 James M. Kouzes and Barry Z. Posner. "*The Five Practices of Exemplary Leadership.*" (San Francisco: Wiley Publishers, 2003): 65.

65 Kouzes and Posner, "*The Five Practices,*" 65.

66 Lester. "LoveBeyondWalls." *LoveBeyondWalls*. Accessed October 19, 2019. http://www.lovebeyondwalls.org/.

67 "He was once homeless. Now he's providing sinks, water and soap to help protect the homeless from the coronavirus." CNN,

March 22, 2020. https://www.cnn.com/2020/03/22/us/sinks-for-homeless-iyw-trnd/index.html

[68] Kouzes and Posner, "*The Five Practices*," 65.

[69] Kouzes and Posner, "*The Five Practices*," 65.

[70] Noel M. Tichy and David O. Ulrich. "SMR Forum: The Leadership Challenge -- A Call for the Transformational Leader." *Sloan Management Review (pre-1986)* 26, no. 1 (1984): 59.

[71] Kouzes and Posner, "The Five Practices," 65.

[72] Kouzes and Posner, "The Five Practices," 65.

[73] Ann-Marie Nienaber, Marcel Hofeditz, and Philipp Daniel Romeike. "Vulnerability and Trust in Leader-Follower Relationships." *Personnel Review* 44, no. 4 (2015): 567.

[74] Warren G. Bennis. *An Invented Life: Reflections on Leadership and Change.* (Boston: Addison Wesley Publishing Company, 1993), 4.

[75] Eva Bianconi, Allison Piovesan, Federica Facchin, Alina Beraudi, Raffaella Casadei, Flavia Frabetti, Lorenza Vitale et al. "An Estimation of the Number of Cells in the Human Body." *Annals of Human Biology* 40, no. 6 (2013): 464.

[76] Warren G. Bennis and Robert Townsend. *On Becoming a Leader.* Vol. 36. (Reading, MA: Addison-Wesley, 1989), 4.

[77] Dictionary, Merriam-Webster. "Merriam-Webster." On-line at http://www. mw. com/home. htm (2002).

[78] Michael G. Brizek Charles G. Partlow, and Lauren "Ashley Nguyen. "S. Truett Cathy: From Young Entrepreneur to a Foodservice Industry Leader." *Journal of Hospitality & Tourism Education* 19, no. 4 (2007): 10.

[79] James M. Kouzes, and Barry Z. Posner. "Ethical Leaders: An Essay about Being in Love." *Journal of Business Ethics* 11, no. 5-6 (1992): 479.

[80] Dictionary, Merriam-Webster. "Merriam-Webster." *On-line at http://www. mw. com/home. htm* (2002).

[81] Dave Ulrich and Norm Smallwood. *Aligning Firm, Leadership, and Personal Brand. Leader to Leader,* (2008), 25.

[82] Dave Ulrich and Norm Smallwood. *Aligning Firm, Leadership, and Personal Brand. Leader to Leader* (New Jersey: Wiley Publishing, 2008): 25.

[83] "Billionaires 2019." Forbes. Forbes Magazine, March 5, 2019. https://www.forbes.com/billionaires/#3fc512e3251c.

[84] "Facebook Users by Country 2019." *Statista.* Accessed September 2019.
https://www.statista.com/statistics/268136/top-15-countries-based-on-number-of-facebook-users/.

[85] Warren Bennis. "The End of Leadership: Exemplary Leadership is Impossible without Full Inclusion, Initiatives, and Cooperation of Followers." *Organizational Dynamics* 28 (1): 71.

[86] Shih Yung Chou. "Millennials in the Workplace: A Conceptual Analysis of Millennials' Leadership and Followership Styles." *International Journal of Human Resource Studies* 2, no. 2 (2012). 74.

[87] M. Sudha and K. Sheena. "Impact of Influencers in Consumer Decision Process: The Fashion Industry." *SCMS Journal of Indian Management* 14, no. 3 (2017): 15.

[88] David M. Mayer. "Servant Leadership and Follower Need Satisfaction." in *Servant Leadership*, (London: Palgrave-Macmillan, 2010): 57.

[89] Christine Porath. "Half of Employees Don't Feel Respected by their Bosses." Harvard Business Review 92 (2014): Accessed October 2019 at https://hbr.org/2014/11/half-of-employees-dont-feel-respected-by-their-bosses

[90] Porath, "Half of Employees, Online.

[91] Porath, "Half of Employees, Online.

[92] John C. Maxwell. *The 21 Irrefutable Laws of Leadership: Follow Them and People Will Follow You.* (Tennessee: Thomas Nelson, 2007): 16.

[93] Yiannis Gabriel. "The Caring Leader: What Followers Expect of Their Leaders and Why." *Leadership* 11, no. 3 (2015): 317.

[94] Joshua B. Wu, Anne S. Tsui, and Angelo J. Kinicki. "Consequences of Differentiated Leadership in Groups." *Academy of Management Journal* 53, no. 1 (2010): 90.

[95] Wu et al, "Consequences of Differentiated Leadership," 92.

96 , H. C. Ngambi. "The Relationship between Leadership and Employee Morale in higher Education." *African Journal of Business Management* 5, no. 3 (2011): 762.

97 Porath, "Half of Employees," Online.

98 Porath, "Half of Employees," Online.

99 Porath, "Half of Employees," Online.

100 Barbara Kellerman. "Cut Off at the Pass: The Limits of Leadership in the 21st Century." *Governance Studies at Brookings".* (Washington, DC: The Brookings Institute, 2012): 8.

101 Bruce E. Winston and Kathleen Patterson. "An Integrative Definition of Leadership." *International Journal of Leadership Studies* 1, no. 2 (2006): 7.

102 James Humes. "The art of communication is the language of leadership." *International Trade* (2008), Online.

103 J. Robert Baum, Edwin A. Locke, and Shelley A. Kirkpatrick. "A Longitudinal Study of the Relation of Vision and Vision Communication to Venture Growth in Entrepreneurial Firms." *Journal of Applied Psychology* 83, no. 1 (1998): 43.

104 J. O. H. N. Velentzas and Georgia Broni. "Communication Cycle: Definition, Process, Models and Examples." *Recent*

Advances in Financial Planning and Product Development (2014): 117.

[105] Pete Yunyongying. "Patient education and counseling: the telephone game revisited?" (2011), 4.

[106] Heather Noel Fedesco. "The Impact of (In)Effective Listening on Interpersonal Interactions." *International Journal of Listening* 29, no. 2 (2015): 103.

[107] E. Hersh, (n.d.). "Using Effective Listening to Improve Leadership in Environmental Health and Safety." [online] *Executive and Continuing Professional Education*. Accessed at: https://www.hsph.harvard.edu/ecpe/listening-to-improve-leadership/.

[108] Larry R Smeltzer. "An Analysis of Receivers' Reactions to Electronically Mediated Communication." *The Journal of Business Communication (1973)* 23, no. 4 (1986): 37.

[109] Hersh, "Using Effective Listening," online.

[110] Robert G. Lord and Douglas J. Brown. "Leadership, Values, and Subordinate Self-Concepts." *The Leadership Quarterly* 12, no. 2 (2001): 136.

[111] Eric LaCore. "Supporting Millennials in the Workplace." *Strategic HR Review* (2015), 156.

[112] Delmatoff and Lazarus, "The Most Effective Leadership Style," 246.

[113] M. Z. Hackman and C. E. Johnson. *Leadership: A Communication Perspective.* (Illinois: Waveland Press, 2013), 28.

[114] J. Delmatoff and I. R. Lazarus. "The Most Effective Leadership Style for the New Landscape of Healthcare." *Journal of Healthcare Management.* (2014) 59(54), 245.

[115] L. A. Grunig, J. E. Grunig, and D. M. Dozier. "Excellence in Public Relations and Communication Management: A Study of Communication Management in Three Countries." *Public Relations Research* (2002). 327.

[116] Ralph Waldo Emerson. Accessed November 2019 at https://www.goodreads.com/quotes/16878-do-not-go-where-the-path-may-lead-go-instead

[117] Joshua H. Williams. "Personality Styles That Influence Organizational Safety." In *ASSE Professional Development Conference and Exposition.* American Society of Safety Engineers, 2002, 32.

[118] Sang M. Lee and Trimi Silvana. "Innovation for Creating a Smart Future." *Journal of Innovation & Knowledge* 3, no. 1 (2018): 4.

[119] Lee and Silvana, "Innovation for Creating a Smart Future," 4.

[120] N. Marsh, M. McAllum and D. Purcell. *Strategic Foresight: The Power of Standing in the Future.* (Melbourne: Crown Content, 2002): 2.

[121] E. Cornish. *Futuring: The Exploration of the Future.* (Maryland: World Future Society, 2004), 147.

[122] M. Lindgren and H. Bandhold. *Scenario Planning.* (New York: Palgrave, 2003),4.

[123] Paul JH Schoemaker. "Scenario Planning: A Tool for Strategic Thinking." *Sloan Management Review* 36, no. 2 (1995): 27.

[124] Schoemaker, "Scenario Planning," 27.

[125] Marsh, McAllum, and Purcell, *Why Strategic Foresight*, 2.

[126] Ronald R. MacDonald. "Uneasy Lies: Language and History in Shakespeare's Lancastrian Tetralogy." *Shakespeare Quarterly* 35, no. 1 (1984): 22-39.

[127] Jennifer Moss Breen. "Leadership Resilience in a VUCA World." In *Visionary Leadership in a Turbulent World: Thriving in the New VUCA Context*, pp. 39-58. (PLACE OF PUBLICATION: Emerald Publishing Limited, 2017), 39.

[128] Salvatore R. Maddi and Deborah M. Khoshaba. "Hardiness Training for Resiliency and Leadership." *Promoting Capabilities to Manage Post-Traumatic Stress: Perspectives on Resilience* (2003): 44.

[129] Alasdair White. *From Comfort Zone to Performance Management.* (Baisy-Thy, England: White & MacLean Publishing, 2009): 2.

[130] White, *From Comfort Zone to Performance Management*, 2.

131 A. Kingsdale. *Kingsdale Advisors.* [website] Kingsdaleadvisors.com. Accessed November 2019 at: http://www.kingsdaleadvisors.com.

132 Sara Hudson. "Overcoming Adversity" *Policy* 32, no. 3 (Spring 2016): 54.

133 Hudson, "Overcoming Adversity," 54.

134 W. Hall. (2017). *WES | Wes Hall Documentary (Extended Version).* [online] YouTube. Available at: https://www.youtube.com/watch?v=gdWqnEMx92I&t=1797 s.

135 Kingsdale, "Kingsdale Advisors," online.

136 Emma Watton, Scott Lichtenstein, and Paul Aitken. "'Won't Get Fooled Again': How Personal Values Shape Leadership Purpose, Behavior, and Legacy." *Journal of Management & Organization* (2019): 416.

137 Watton, Lichtenstein, and Aitken, "Won't Get Fooled Again," 415.

CPSIA information can be obtained
at www.ICGtesting.com
Printed in the USA
LVHW040253120723
752152LV00002B/133